The Truth Behind the Creation Story

Alex Telman

Published by Alex Telman, 2024.

THE TRUTH BEHIND THE CREATION STORY

First edition. October 10, 2024.

ISBN: 979-8227327420

Written by Alex Telman.

Table of Contents

Table of Contents

Author's Note

Dear Readers,

As you embark on this exploration of the Creation Story, reincarnation, and the intricate web of chakras, I want to take a moment to share my intention behind this book and what it means to me.

In a world often dominated by materialism and fast-paced living, I believe it is essential to reconnect with the deeper narratives that shape our existence. The themes of creation and reincarnation are not merely ancient tales; they are profound reflections of our spiritual journey and the transformative experiences that define who we are. They resonate with the universal questions that many of us grapple with: Who am I? Why am I here? What is my purpose?

My hope is to illuminate these connections, offering you insights that encourage self-reflection and growth. As we traverse the stages of creation and the development of our chakras, we uncover the rich layers of our human experience. Each chakra serves as a gateway to understanding our emotions, our identities, and our relationships with the world around us. By recognizing how these energy centers correspond to the Creation Story and the cycle of reincarnation, we can cultivate a deeper awareness of ourselves and our interconnectedness with all life.

This journey is as much personal as it is collective. It reflects my own explorations, questions, and discoveries over the years. I have often found solace in understanding that every struggle, every moment of joy, and every lesson learned contributes to the evolution of my spirit. I invite you to embrace this perspective, allowing it to transform how you view your own experiences.

As you read, may you find threads of connection that resonate with your own life story. May you uncover insights that inspire you to embrace your journey of reincarnation with courage and curiosity. And may you come to see the Creation Story not just as a historical account, but as a living narrative that continuously shapes our understanding of existence. I encourage you to approach these concepts with an open heart and mind. Allow yourself to be curious, to question, and to explore. The beauty of this journey lies not just in the destination but in the unfolding path that leads us there.

Thank you for joining me on this profound journey. Together, let's explore the depths of creation, the cycles of rebirth, and the transformative power of our energy systems. May this book serve as a guiding light on your path toward self-discovery, healing, and spiritual awakening.

With gratitude and excitement,

Alex

Introduction

What if the ancient story of creation is not just a tale of beginnings, but a metaphor for a profound journey of the soul through reincarnation and energy transformation? In this book, we will explore the intricate connections between the Creation Story, the cycle of reincarnation, and the human energy system known as chakras. Each element reflects a deeper understanding of our existence and purpose, inviting us to explore not only where we come from, but who we are becoming.

From the moment of conception to the final breath, our lives can be viewed as a tapestry woven with threads of spiritual evolution, emotional growth, and transformative experiences. The Creation Story serves as a foundational narrative that resonates across cultures, illustrating not just how the universe was formed, but also offering insights into the human experience. By viewing this story through the lens of reincarnation, we can appreciate life as a continuous cycle of learning, growth, and renewal.

Reincarnation posits that our souls are on a journey through multiple lifetimes, each serving as a chapter in our spiritual evolution. This journey shapes our identities, challenges our perceptions, and ultimately guides us toward self-actualization. Just as the Creation Story unfolds in stages, so too does our journey through life, each incarnation providing unique lessons and opportunities for growth.

At the core of this exploration is the chakra system—an intricate framework that maps our energy centers and emotional states. Each chakra represents different aspects of our being, from the instinctual and grounded nature of the root chakra to the higher consciousness associated with the crown chakra. Understanding how these energy centers relate to the themes of creation and reincarnation can illuminate our paths and empower us to navigate life with greater awareness.

This book will delve into each day of creation, paralleling it with the experiences of the soul in the womb and the development of the chakras. For instance, just as light was created on the first day, illuminating the universe, so too does the soul emerge into awareness within the nurturing environment of the womb. Each chapter will explore the nuanced interplay between these themes, offering readers a rich tapestry of insights.

Moreover, we will examine the psychological dimensions of these concepts, drawing upon theories such as Jungian archetypes and developmental psychology. This exploration will reveal how creation, reincarnation, and energy dynamics manifest in our personal identities, transformations, and quests for self-actualization.

As you embark on this journey through the pages of this book, I invite you to approach it with an open heart and mind. Allow the insights shared here to resonate with your own experiences and aspirations. Together, we will uncover the profound wisdom that lies within the story of creation, illuminating our paths toward understanding ourselves and the universe in which we exist.

In the end, this is not merely a story; it is an invitation to explore the sacred dance of existence, where every heartbeat, every breath, and every thought contributes to the magnificent tapestry of life. Let us begin this journey of discovery together.

The journey of existence is one of profound complexity and beauty, intricately woven into the fabric of our very being. As we explore the ancient narrative of creation, particularly in the context of the biblical account of Genesis, we uncover deep parallels with the experiences of the spirit in the womb and the formation of the human energy system, notably the chakras. This book aims to illuminate these connections, offering insights into how the act of creation resonates with our spiritual journey and the development of our energetic anatomy.

The Act of Creation: A Divine Blueprint

In the beginning, as described in Genesis, God initiated a magnificent process of creation, transforming chaos into order, darkness into light. This sacred narrative reveals not just the physical formation of the universe but also the spiritual essence underlying it. Each day of creation presents a sequence that can be likened to the unfolding of life itself—an archetype for the soul's journey through various stages of existence. As we reflect on this act of creation, we can draw parallels to the sacred experience of the spirit entering the womb, where life begins in a realm of protection and potential.

The Spirit in the Womb: A Sacred Sanctuary

The womb serves as a nurturing environment, a sacred sanctuary where the spirit begins its earthly journey. Here, in the protective embrace of the mother, the soul prepares to manifest in the physical realm. This process mirrors the divine act of creation, where each aspect of existence is meticulously crafted and infused with purpose. Just as God breathed life into the world, the spirit in the womb begins to awaken to the experiences that will shape its earthly existence. It is within this sacred space that the energies of the chakras begin to develop, forming the foundation for our emotional, mental, and spiritual lives.

The Human Energy System: A Divine Reflection

As the spirit inhabits the womb, it begins to form a complex energy system that includes the chakras—seven primary energy centers that correspond to different aspects of our being. Each chakra represents unique qualities and experiences, much like the stages of creation described in Genesis. From the grounding energy of the Root Chakra to the spiritual transcendence of the Crown Chakra, these energy centers reflect the divine blueprint of creation. They encapsulate the journey of the spirit from its origins to its earthly manifestation, echoing the sacred process of creation itself.

Connecting Creation and Energy

The correlation between the act of creation and the experiences of the spirit in the womb offers a rich tapestry of understanding. Each day of creation can be seen as a distinct phase in the development of the chakras, symbolizing the emergence of consciousness and the unfolding of our spiritual identity. As we navigate through the teachings of this book, we will explore how these connections deepen our understanding of our existence, our purpose, and the intricate interplay between the physical and the spiritual realms.

A Journey of Discovery

This exploration is not just an academic endeavor; it is an invitation to embark on a journey of self-discovery and spiritual awakening. By understanding how the creation narrative parallels the experiences of the spirit and the development of the chakra system, we can gain insights into our own lives and the sacred journey we each undertake. As we reflect on our individual paths, we will uncover the wisdom of our experiences, empowering us to embrace our divine nature and the interconnectedness of all life.

In the pages that follow, we will delve into each day of creation, relating it to the experiences of the spirit in the womb and the unfolding of the human energy system. Together, we will uncover the profound truths that lie at the intersection of creation, existence, and spiritual growth. Through this exploration, may we all find greater awareness, healing, and connection to the divine essence that flows through us, illuminating our journey as we navigate the intricate dance of life.

The Essence of Creation and Spirituality

The narrative of creation is not merely a historical account; it serves as a profound metaphor for our spiritual evolution. Each day of creation embodies stages that reflect not only the formation of the physical world but also the inner workings of our souls as they prepare to embark on their earthly journeys. Just as the universe was shaped through divine intention, so too are our lives crafted through the energies we cultivate and the experiences we embrace.

Embracing the Divine Connection

As we move forward in this exploration, we will dive deeper into how the act of creation aligns with the soul's journey through the womb and the unfolding of the chakras. This alignment invites us to reflect on our own experiences and recognize the divine thread that weaves through every aspect of our existence. Each chakra serves as a gateway to understanding our emotions, thoughts, and spiritual aspirations. By aligning these energies with the creation story, we open ourselves to greater insights and a more profound connection to the universe.

The Journey Ahead

Throughout this book, we will explore each day of creation in relation to the soul's experience in the womb and the development of the chakras. We will examine how each stage of creation informs our understanding of our own spiritual journey, emphasizing the significance of nurturing our energy centers and recognizing the divine nature within us.

As we delve into these teachings, we will engage with practical exercises, reflective questions, and meditative practices designed to deepen our awareness of these connections. This journey is not only about understanding the theoretical aspects but also about embodying the wisdom gained through experience.

Invitation to Reflect

I invite you, dear reader, to approach this journey with an open heart and a curious mind. As we explore the sacred intersections between creation, spiritual experience, and the energy system, allow yourself to reflect on your own life and the ways in which these themes resonate with you. Each chapter is designed to guide you deeper into your own understanding, fostering a sense of empowerment and connection to the divine.

As you read, consider how the process of creation mirrors your own journey. How do the energies of your chakras reflect the stages of your development? In what ways can the teachings of creation inspire you to nurture your spirit and embrace your unique path?

This book is more than a scholarly examination of creation and spirituality; it is an invitation to embark on a transformative journey. By exploring the connections between the act of creation, the experiences of the spirit in the womb, and the development of the chakras, we come to understand that we are all part of a greater cosmic narrative. As we engage with this narrative, we can awaken to the divinity within ourselves and recognize our interconnectedness with all life.

May this exploration bring you insights, healing, and a deeper connection to the essence of creation that flows through us all. Together, let us journey into the depths of existence, discovering the sacred truths that illuminate our path and enrich our spiritual lives.

Genesis 1

In Genesis 1, the narrative unfolds with God creating the universe in an orderly and purposeful manner. Each day brings new elements into existence—light, sky, land, vegetation, animals, and finally, humanity. This creation process emphasizes a structured progression, where each step builds upon the previous one, culminating in a harmonious and balanced world. The act of creation is portrayed as intentional, with God bestowing life and purpose upon His creations.

Now, let's consider reincarnation, which is often viewed as the soul's journey through multiple lifetimes. In this perspective, the spirit realm serves as a place of existence before entering a physical form. Each incarnation represents a new opportunity for growth, learning, and evolution, akin to how God's creation in Genesis unfolds in stages. Just as God introduces different elements to the world, the soul, through reincarnation, explores various experiences and challenges, contributing to its overall development.

Both processes reflect a cycle of renewal and transformation. In Genesis, the world is created with inherent potential and purpose, leading to a vibrant and diverse ecosystem. Similarly, when a soul reincarnates, it brings the lessons and experiences from past lives, aiming to fulfill its potential in a new physical existence. This cyclical nature—creation in Genesis and reincarnation—highlights the idea of continual growth and evolution.

Moreover, in Genesis, God's creation is ultimately deemed "good," reflecting a sense of inherent value in existence. In reincarnation, each life is viewed as an opportunity for the soul to engage with its environment, learn, and contribute positively to the world. Just as God's creation involves nurturing relationships among His creations, the reincarnated soul is often seen as interconnected with others, fostering empathy and understanding.

Both Genesis 1 and the process of reincarnation speak to a deliberate and meaningful unfolding of existence. They emphasize growth, interconnectedness, and the potential for transformation—whether through divine creation or the journey of the soul. This analogy invites deeper reflection on the nature of life, purpose, and the ongoing quest for understanding within both spiritual and physical realms.

Day 1: Correlation between day 1 creation and the experience of the soul in the womb

The correlation between the first day of creation, when God creates light, and the experience of the soul in the womb is rich with metaphorical significance. Here are several key points that illustrate this relationship:

1. Emergence of Light: On the first day, God said, "Let there be light," bringing illumination to the void. This act symbolizes the awakening of consciousness and awareness. Similarly, the soul's journey in the womb represents a phase of awakening, where the soul begins to connect with the physical body and the world around it. Just as light dispels darkness, the soul's entry into the womb signifies a transition from the formless realm of spirit to the structured environment of physical existence.

2. Formation of Identity: Light represents clarity and definition, enabling the differentiation of forms. In the womb, the developing fetus begins to form its identity, gradually distinguishing itself from its surroundings. This mirrors the soul's journey of self-discovery, where it begins to understand its individuality and purpose within the context of a new life.

3. Connection to the Divine: Light is often associated with divine presence and guidance. The soul in the womb is still closely connected to the spiritual realm, experiencing a sense of unity with the divine. This connection provides a nurturing environment for the soul, much like the light that illuminates and guides. The womb can be seen as a sacred space where the soul is enveloped in divine love and protection.

4. Potential and Possibility: The creation of light signifies the beginning of possibilities and the unfolding of creation. In the womb, the soul is filled with potential, ready to embark on a journey of growth, learning, and exploration. Just as light allows for the perception of the world, the womb serves as a gateway for the soul to engage with life, full of opportunities for development.

5. Transition from Chaos to Order: Before the creation of light, there was chaos and formlessness. The act of creating light symbolizes the establishment of order and purpose. The womb is a space where the soul experiences a structured environment that fosters growth and development. This transition from chaos to

order reflects the soul's journey of coming into form and beginning its life in the physical realm.

6. Illumination of Existence: Light serves as a metaphor for understanding and knowledge. In the womb, the soul begins to absorb experiences that will shape its understanding of existence. This early stage of life is foundational for the soul, laying the groundwork for its future interactions and experiences in the world.

7. Symbol of Hope: The creation of light represents hope and new beginnings. For the soul in the womb, this phase is filled with promise and anticipation. Just as light brings warmth and clarity, the womb nurtures the soul, preparing it for the journey ahead and instilling a sense of hope for the life that is about to unfold.

The correlation between the first day of creation and the experience of the soul in the womb highlights themes of emergence, identity, connection to the divine, potential, and transformation. Both signify the beginning of a journey, marked by light and illumination, guiding the soul as it prepares to enter the world. This metaphorical link emphasizes the sacred nature of both creation and the developmental process, celebrating the profound mystery of life and existence.

Day 1 Chakra

The energy chakra that corresponds to Day 1 of Creation, when God created light and separated it from darkness, is the Root Chakra (Muladhara). Here's an explanation of how they relate:

1. Foundation of Existence

- Root Chakra: The Root Chakra is the foundation of our energetic system, relating to basic survival, stability, and grounding. It represents our connection to the earth and our physical existence.

- Day 1 Creation: The creation of light signifies the very beginning of existence. Light is often seen as a source of life and clarity, illuminating the path for all creation to follow. Just as the Root Chakra establishes our connection to life, Day 1 sets the stage for all subsequent creation.

2. Separation and Duality

- Root Chakra: This chakra is associated with the duality of existence, such as safety vs. danger, stability vs. instability. It embodies the balance between these opposites.

- Day 1 Creation: The separation of light from darkness introduces the concept of duality in the universe. This act symbolizes the fundamental distinctions that govern our reality, such as good vs. evil, clarity vs. confusion, and consciousness vs. unconsciousness. The Root Chakra facilitates our understanding of these dualities in our physical lives.

3. Energy and Vitality

- Root Chakra: This chakra is linked to our life force energy, vitality, and the primal instincts necessary for survival. It governs our physical needs and desires.

- Day 1 Creation: Light can be viewed as a representation of energy and vitality. By creating light, God instills the universe with the energy necessary for all life forms. This mirrors how the Root Chakra provides the foundational energy that sustains our physical body and spirit.

4. Awareness and Presence

- Root Chakra: Being anchored in the present and aware of our surroundings is crucial for the health of the Root Chakra. It encourages mindfulness and a sense of belonging.

- Day 1 Creation: The introduction of light brings awareness and consciousness into the void, allowing for perception and understanding of the universe. This awareness parallels the Root Chakra's role in helping us stay present and connected to our physical reality.

5. Connection to Earth

- Root Chakra: It embodies our connection to the earth, grounding us and giving us a sense of security.

- Day 1 Creation: The act of creating light can symbolize the initial energy that connects all of creation to the earth. Just as the Root Chakra connects us to our physical environment, the creation of light signifies the emergence of a world where life can flourish.

The Root Chakra corresponds with Day 1 of Creation as it establishes the foundational aspects of existence, survival, and duality. Just as light illuminates and gives life to the universe, the Root Chakra grounds us in our physical reality, fostering stability and awareness as we navigate the world. This connection highlights the importance of understanding our roots in both a spiritual and physical sense.

Day 1 Reincarnation

The correlation between the creation of light in Genesis 1 and the concept of reincarnation can yield some profound insights.

In Genesis 1:3, God proclaims, "Let there be light," and light is created, signifying the beginning of the universe's transformation from chaos to order. This act of creating light can be seen as a metaphor for awareness, enlightenment, and the initiation of life itself. Light is often associated with knowledge, clarity, and the awakening of consciousness.

Now, let's connect this to reincarnation. In many spiritual beliefs, reincarnation represents the soul's journey through different physical forms to gain experiences, learn lessons, and ultimately evolve. Each new life can be viewed as a new opportunity for the soul to bring light—awareness and understanding—into the world. Just as God's creation of light brings clarity to the cosmos, the reincarnated soul brings its accumulated wisdom and insights from previous lives into its new existence.

Furthermore, light in spiritual contexts often symbolizes purity and the divine essence within each being. When a soul reincarnates, it is believed to carry the essence of its past experiences, including the lessons learned and the challenges faced. This essence can illuminate the path forward, guiding the soul in its new life. In this way, the act of reincarnation is akin to the continuous emergence of light; with each life, the soul has the chance to shine brighter, embodying greater understanding and compassion.

Additionally, light serves as a fundamental element of creation, allowing for the existence of life as we know it. Similarly, the process of reincarnation suggests that the soul is never extinguished but instead continues to evolve and adapt. Each life serves as a vessel for the soul's light, with the potential to illuminate both its own path and the lives of others around it. This reflects the interconnectedness of all beings, as the light of one soul can influence and uplift the collective.

The creation of light in Genesis parallels the concept of reincarnation in that both signify the emergence of consciousness, awareness, and potential. Light represents the divine spark within, guiding the soul through its journey across different lifetimes. Just as light dispels darkness and brings clarity, each reincarnation offers the opportunity for growth, learning, and the eventual realization of one's true essence.

Day 1 Nuanced

Root Chakra (Muladhara): A Nuanced Perspective in Relation to Creation and Reincarnation

The Root Chakra, or Muladhara, is the first energy center in the chakra system, fundamentally linked to our sense of security, survival, and connection to the physical world. It is the foundation upon which our entire energetic system is built and embodies themes of grounding, stability, and primal instincts. In the context of the creation story and the process of reincarnation, the Root Chakra plays a pivotal role, emphasizing our connection to the Earth and our physical existence. Here's a nuanced exploration of its significance:

1. Foundation of Existence

- Creation of the Physical Realm: In the creation narrative, the initial act of bringing light into the void represents the birth of existence itself. The Root Chakra mirrors this foundational aspect, representing our primal connection to the Earth and our physical bodies. Just as God established the physical world, the Root Chakra grounds us, anchoring our souls in the material plane. This connection is vital for our journey through reincarnation, as it emphasizes the importance of being present in our physical bodies and the reality of our experiences.

2. Security and Survival

- Basic Needs and Instincts: The Root Chakra is intimately linked to our survival instincts and basic needs—food, shelter, safety, and stability. In the creation story, these elements are reflected in the establishment of the Earth as a place for life to flourish. In reincarnation, the Root Chakra represents the soul's need to navigate physical existence, ensuring that it can thrive in each new life. This energy supports the notion that our survival is not just a physical necessity but also a spiritual journey, as we learn to balance our earthly needs with our spiritual aspirations.

3. Connection to Ancestry and Heritage

- Roots of Family and Lineage: The Root Chakra embodies our connection to our ancestors and heritage, symbolizing the familial ties that ground us. In the context of creation, this connection reflects the continuity of life and the importance of lineage. Each reincarnation is influenced by our familial history, shaping our experiences and lessons. The Root Chakra encourages us to honor our roots and understand how they inform our current life, emphasizing the significance of lineage in the ongoing journey of the soul.

4. Grounding in the Present Moment

- Awareness of the Physical Experience: The creation narrative emphasizes the establishment of the Earth and its resources, inviting us to engage with the physical world. The Root Chakra reminds us to ground ourselves in the present moment, fostering awareness of our surroundings and physical sensations. In the reincarnation process, this grounding is essential for integrating our experiences and learning from them. By cultivating a strong Root Chakra, we can navigate life's challenges with resilience and a sense of belonging.

5. Stability in Transition

- Navigating Life Changes: The Root Chakra provides the stability necessary to navigate the transitions inherent in reincarnation. Each new life brings with it challenges and opportunities for growth. In the creation story, the establishment of the Earth as a stable environment mirrors the Root Chakra's role in providing a sense of security during times of change. This stability allows us to face the uncertainties of life with courage and adaptability, embracing the lessons each reincarnation offers.

6. Embodiment of Primal Energy

- Vital Life Force: The Root Chakra embodies the primal energy that fuels life. In the context of creation, this energy is evident in the vibrant ecosystem established by God. In reincarnation, the Root Chakra represents the life force that animates our physical bodies, reminding us of the sacredness of life itself. This energy encourages us to honor our physical existence and appreciate the intricate web of life that connects us all.

7. Connection to Nature and the Earth

- Environmental Awareness: The Root Chakra fosters a deep connection to nature and the Earth, highlighting our role as stewards of the planet. In the creation narrative, God's act of forming the Earth symbolizes the intrinsic relationship between humanity and the environment. In reincarnation, this connection reinforces the idea that our physical existence is intertwined with the natural world. By nurturing our Root Chakra, we can cultivate a greater appreciation for the Earth and our responsibility to protect and preserve it.

8. Balance Between Body and Spirit

- Holistic Existence: The Root Chakra serves as a reminder of the balance between our physical and spiritual selves. In the creation story, the physical world is a manifestation of divine intention. In the process of reincarnation, this balance becomes crucial, as our spiritual journey is experienced through our physical bodies. By grounding ourselves in the Root Chakra, we honor both our earthly existence and our spiritual aspirations, creating a harmonious integration of body and spirit.

The Root Chakra offers profound insights into the connections between the creation story and the process of reincarnation. Through its emphasis on grounding, survival, ancestry, and the sacredness of life, the Root Chakra serves as the foundation for our journey through existence. It reminds us of the importance of our physical bodies and the lessons we learn from our earthly experiences. By cultivating the energy of the Root Chakra, we deepen our understanding of ourselves and our place in the cosmos, embracing the beautiful interplay between creation and reincarnation.

Day 2: Correlation between day 2 creation and the experience of the soul in the womb

The correlation between the second day of creation, when God separates the waters to create the sky, and the experience of the soul in the womb can be explored through several meaningful parallels:

1. Separation and Structure: On the second day, God creates the sky by separating the waters (sky) above from the waters below. This act of division brings order and structure to what was previously chaotic. Similarly, in the womb, the soul experiences a structured environment as it separates from the formless spirit realm. The womb acts as a protective boundary, providing a defined space for the soul's development, much like the sky creates a defined separation in the cosmos.

2. Nurturing Environment: The sky serves as a protective barrier that holds the waters, allowing life to flourish on earth. In the womb, the amniotic fluid acts similarly, cushioning and protecting the developing fetus. This nurturing environment is essential for growth and development, paralleling how the sky's presence supports life on Earth by regulating conditions and shielding from external elements.

3. Connection to the Elemental: The waters represent emotions and the subconscious, while the sky embodies the realm of thought and spirit. In the womb, the soul exists in a state where it begins to engage with both its emotional and spiritual dimensions. This phase allows for the integration of these aspects, preparing the soul for the emotional experiences of life outside the womb.

4. Awareness and Perception: Just as the sky allows for light to penetrate and create visibility, the womb facilitates the initial stages of perception for the soul. As the fetus develops, it becomes increasingly aware of its surroundings, beginning to perceive sensations, sounds, and rhythms. This emerging awareness mirrors the clarity and openness that the sky represents, allowing the soul to prepare for its forthcoming journey.

5. Symbol of Growth and Potential: The separation of waters creates space for life to thrive on land, emphasizing growth and potential. Similarly, the womb is a place where the soul is nurtured and prepared for its emergence into the world. This phase is critical for the soul, allowing it to develop physically,

emotionally, and spiritually, much like the creation of the sky enables the flourishing of terrestrial life.

6. Transition and Transformation: The act of creating the sky symbolizes a significant transformation in the cosmos, moving from chaos to order. In the womb, the soul undergoes its own transformation as it grows and develops, preparing for the transition into physical existence. This phase represents a critical juncture, where the soul evolves from a potential being to one ready to engage with the world.

7. Symbol of Hope and Possibility: The sky often represents hope, aspiration, and the infinite possibilities of life. In the womb, the soul is filled with potential, symbolizing the hope and promise of a new life. Just as the sky opens up to vast horizons, the womb prepares the soul for the limitless opportunities that lie ahead.

The correlation between the second day of creation and the experience of the soul in the womb underscores themes of separation, structure, nurturing, and growth. Both processes reflect a movement from chaos to order, providing a foundation for life and development. The sky, as a protective and supportive element, parallels the womb's role in nurturing the soul, emphasizing the sacredness of both creation and the developmental journey of life.

Day 2 chakra

The energy chakra that corresponds to Day 2 of Creation, when God created the sky and separated the waters, is the Sacral Chakra (Svadhisthana). Here's how they relate:

1. Creativity and Fluidity

- Sacral Chakra: The Sacral Chakra is associated with creativity, fluidity, and the flow of emotions. It governs our ability to create and engage with the world in a dynamic way.

- Day 2 Creation: The creation of the sky signifies the establishment of a space for expression and movement. Just as the sky allows for various forms of weather and atmospheric phenomena, the Sacral Chakra encourages creative expression and the exploration of emotions.

2. Separation and Boundaries

- Sacral Chakra: This chakra helps establish healthy boundaries in relationships and our emotional life. It allows us to differentiate between self and others, facilitating connection without losing identity.

- Day 2 Creation: The separation of the waters by the sky introduces a structure to the universe. This act reflects the need for boundaries that are essential for growth and development. The Sacral Chakra embodies this need for emotional boundaries and personal space.

3. Emotional Depth

- Sacral Chakra: Linked to our emotional well-being, the Sacral Chakra encourages us to explore our feelings and desires.

- Day 2 Creation: The sky, as a vast expanse above the waters, represents the potential for emotional depth and the complexities of human experience. It creates a space for emotions to be expressed freely, just as the Sacral Chakra allows us to embrace and navigate our emotional landscape.

4. Connection to Water

- Sacral Chakra: Water is a significant element associated with the Sacral Chakra, symbolizing emotions, intuition, and the subconscious.

- Day 2 Creation: The act of separating the waters can be seen as the establishment of a nurturing environment where life can thrive. The sky above creates a container for this water, similar to how the Sacral Chakra governs the flow of emotional energy and the nurturing aspects of creativity.

5. Flexibility and Adaptability

- Sacral Chakra: This chakra promotes adaptability and the ability to go with the flow of life.

- Day 2 Creation: The creation of the sky provides the necessary conditions for weather patterns and changes in the environment. This reflects the need for flexibility and adaptability in our emotional responses and creative pursuits, which the Sacral Chakra encourages.

The Sacral Chakra correlates with Day 2 of Creation through its focus on creativity, emotional depth, and the importance of boundaries. The separation of the waters by the sky symbolizes the establishment of a nurturing environment where creativity and emotional exploration can flourish, just as the Sacral Chakra enables us to embrace our feelings and express ourselves authentically. This connection emphasizes the significance of balance between structure and fluidity in both the universe and our emotional lives.

Day 2 Reincarnation

The second day of creation in Genesis describes God separating the waters and creating the sky, which serves as a barrier between the earthly realm and the waters above. This act of creating the sky can be correlated with the process of reincarnation in several meaningful ways.

1. Separation and Distinction: On the second day, the act of creating the sky represents the establishment of boundaries and distinctions—between the waters below and the heavens above. Similarly, reincarnation involves a process of transition where the soul moves from the spiritual realm into the physical body. This transition creates a distinction between the two states of existence: the ethereal, spiritual dimension and the material world. Just as the sky provides a framework for life on Earth, the reincarnation process establishes a new context for the soul's journey, allowing it to engage with and learn from the physical plane.

2. Protection and Nurturing: The sky serves not only as a divider but also as a protective layer, shielding the earth from chaos. In the context of reincarnation, this protective aspect can be seen as the guidance and support that the soul receives during its earthly journey. The soul, while in a physical body, is nurtured by the experiences and lessons offered by life. The sky, therefore, symbolizes the nurturing aspect of the spiritual realm, providing the soul with the necessary environment to grow and evolve through various incarnations.

3. The Connection Between Realms: The sky acts as a bridge between the earth and the divine, facilitating communication and connection between the two realms. In reincarnation, the soul maintains a link to its spiritual origins while navigating the physical world. This connection can be viewed as the soul's innate awareness of its purpose and the lessons it must learn in each lifetime. Just as the sky connects the heavens with the earth, the soul's journey through reincarnation connects its past experiences with its current life, influencing its growth and development.

4. Awareness and Perspective: The sky provides a broader perspective, enabling beings on Earth to look up and connect with something greater than themselves. This aspect mirrors the idea that reincarnation offers the soul opportunities to gain wisdom and insight from various life experiences. Each

life adds to the soul's understanding of existence, much like how gazing at the vast sky can inspire reflection and contemplation. The process of reincarnation encourages the soul to rise above its challenges and recognize the interconnectedness of all life, akin to observing the expanse of the sky that unites all beings under its canopy.

The creation of the sky on the second day of Genesis can be analogously viewed as a reflection of the reincarnation process. It signifies the establishment of boundaries and connections between realms, the protection and nurturing of the soul during its journey, and the broader perspective that comes from understanding the interplay between the spiritual and physical worlds. Both serve as frameworks for growth, learning, and the pursuit of higher awareness.

Day 2 Nuanced

Sacral Chakra (Svadhisthana): A Nuanced Perspective in Relation to Creation and Reincarnation:

The Sacral Chakra, or Svadhisthana, is the second energy center in the chakra system and is intimately connected to emotions, creativity, pleasure, and relationships. It embodies our capacity for desire, emotional connection, and the appreciation of life's pleasures. In the context of the creation story and the process of reincarnation, the Sacral Chakra highlights the themes of creation, fluidity, and the intricate dance of relationships. Here's a nuanced exploration of its significance:

1. Emotional Creation and Fluidity

- The Birth of Life: In the creation narrative, the act of creation is often imbued with emotion and intention. The Sacral Chakra represents this fluidity and the emotional energy that fuels creation. Just as God created living beings, the Sacral Chakra encourages us to embrace our emotions and desires as vital forces that drive our creativity. In reincarnation, this energy supports the soul's journey, allowing it to express itself through relationships and experiences that foster growth.

2. Desire as a Creative Force

- The Role of Desire in Creation: The Sacral Chakra is deeply connected to our desires, which can serve as powerful motivators for action and creativity. In the creation story, God's desires manifest as the natural world and all living things. Similarly, in the reincarnation process, our desires play a crucial role in shaping our experiences and choices. They guide us toward fulfilling our purpose and can inspire us to create and nurture life in various forms.

3. Relationships and Interconnection

- The Web of Life: The Sacral Chakra emphasizes the importance of relationships and emotional connections. In the context of creation, the interconnectedness of all living beings mirrors the relational dynamics emphasized by the Sacral Chakra. Reincarnation reinforces this concept, as each soul engages with others, learning through interactions and shared experiences. These relationships provide opportunities for healing, growth, and the exploration of deep emotional themes, highlighting the necessity of connection in the journey of the soul.

4. Embracing Change and Transformation

- The Cycle of Life: The fluid nature of the Sacral Chakra represents the ongoing cycle of creation and transformation. In the creation story, life evolves and adapts, much like the transformative experiences we encounter during reincarnation. The Sacral Chakra encourages us to embrace change, understanding that every experience—be it joyful or challenging—contributes to our emotional and spiritual development. This acceptance allows us to navigate the ups and downs of life with grace.

5. Pleasure and Joy as Spiritual Pathways

- Finding Divinity in Pleasure: The Sacral Chakra invites us to explore pleasure, creativity, and the joy of existence. In the creation narrative, God's creation is deemed "good," reflecting the inherent beauty and pleasure found in the world. In reincarnation, embracing joy and pleasure can elevate our spiritual experience and connection to the divine. The Sacral Chakra teaches us that our emotional states, particularly those related to joy, are essential for holistic well-being and spiritual growth.

6. Creative Expression and Manifestation

- Bringing Ideas to Life: The Sacral Chakra is a powerful center for creativity and self-expression. In the context of the creation story, the act of creation itself is a manifestation of divine ideas into the physical realm. In reincarnation, the Sacral Chakra helps us channel our creative energies, allowing us to express our unique gifts and contribute to the tapestry of life. This expression can take many forms, from art to relationships, nurturing the creative potential inherent in each soul.

7. Healing Through Emotional Release

- Processing Past Experiences: The Sacral Chakra also addresses the need for emotional healing. In the reincarnation process, unresolved emotions and past traumas can influence our current experiences. The creation narrative emphasizes the importance of balance and harmony in nature, mirroring our need to heal and integrate our emotional experiences. By processing these emotions, we create space for new experiences and personal growth, allowing the cycle of life to continue.

8. Balancing Dualities

- Harmony Between Masculine and Feminine: The Sacral Chakra is a space where the masculine and feminine energies can find balance. In the creation story, the dualities of existence—light and dark, land and sea—represent this interplay. In reincarnation, understanding and harmonizing these energies within ourselves allows for a more holistic experience. Embracing both sides fosters creativity and deeper connections with others, enriching our journey through life.

The Sacral Chakra offers profound insights into the connections between the creation story and the process of reincarnation. Through the themes of emotional fluidity, desire, creativity, and relationships, the Sacral Chakra embodies the essence of life's journey. It reminds us that our emotions and connections are vital to our growth and evolution, both as individuals and as part of the greater whole. As we cultivate the energy of the Sacral Chakra, we deepen our understanding of ourselves and our purpose, embracing the beautiful complexity of existence as we navigate the cycles of creation and reincarnation.

Day 3: Correlation between day 3 creation and the experience of the soul in the womb

The correlation between the third day of creation, when God gathers the waters to create dry land and brings forth plants and trees, and the experience of the soul in the womb can be explored through several meaningful parallels:

1. Emergence and Formation: On the third day, God separates the waters to reveal dry land, symbolizing emergence and the establishment of a foundation for life. In the womb, the soul is similarly in a formative stage, emerging from the spiritual realm into the physical world. This phase is crucial for laying the groundwork for the soul's future experiences and growth.

2. Nurturing Growth: The creation of plants and trees represents the potential for life and sustenance. Just as vegetation provides nourishment and supports the ecosystem, the womb provides essential nutrients and support for the developing fetus. This nurturing environment allows the soul to thrive, paralleling how plants root themselves in the earth and grow towards the light.

3. Connection to Life: The act of bringing forth vegetation signifies a connection to life and the natural world. Within the womb, the soul begins to form an intrinsic connection to its physical body and the life it will soon inhabit. This bond is essential for the soul's understanding of its purpose and place within the larger tapestry of existence.

4. Symbol of Stability and Security: The establishment of dry land provides stability and security in the creation narrative. Similarly, the womb offers a secure environment for the developing soul, safeguarding it from external chaos. This stability is vital for the soul's preparation for its journey into the world, allowing it to grow and develop without fear.

5. Diversity and Uniqueness: The variety of plants and trees created on the third day symbolizes diversity and the uniqueness of life. In the womb, the soul experiences its individuality, gradually becoming aware of its distinct personality and traits. This phase of development fosters the soul's uniqueness, preparing it for its specific role in life.

6. Interdependence: The relationship between land and vegetation illustrates the interdependence of all life forms. In the womb, the soul begins to understand its connection to others and the world around it. This foundational

understanding is crucial as the soul prepares to engage with a community and form relationships in its future life.

7. Growth Towards Light: Plants are known for their tendency to grow towards the light, symbolizing hope and aspiration. Within the womb, the soul is on a journey of growth and development, instinctively reaching towards the light of life. This growth mirrors the plants' pursuit of sunlight, representing the soul's inherent desire to thrive and fulfill its purpose.

8. Preparation for Life: The creation of a habitat for living beings underscores the idea of preparation for life. In the womb, the soul is being prepared for its earthly journey, developing the physical and emotional tools necessary for navigating the complexities of existence. This preparation phase is essential for ensuring that the soul is equipped to face life's challenges.

The correlation between the third day of creation and the experience of the soul in the womb highlights themes of emergence, nurturing growth, stability, and the interdependence of life. Both processes reflect the importance of forming a solid foundation for existence, fostering the soul's development and preparation for its unique journey in the world. Just as the land and vegetation create a rich environment for life, the womb provides a sacred space for the soul to grow and thrive.

Day 3 Chakra

The energy chakra that corresponds to Day 3 of Creation, when God gathered the waters to reveal dry land and brought forth plants and trees, is the Solar Plexus Chakra (Manipura). Here's how they relate:

1. Personal Power and Will

- Solar Plexus Chakra: This chakra is associated with personal power, self-confidence, and the ability to assert one's will. It governs our sense of identity and our ability to take action in the world.

- Day 3 Creation: The emergence of dry land symbolizes the solid foundation upon which life can grow and thrive. Just as the Solar Plexus Chakra empowers us to stand strong and pursue our goals, the revelation of land provides the necessary stability for plants and trees to flourish.

2. Growth and Vitality

- Solar Plexus Chakra: This chakra is linked to energy, vitality, and growth. It encourages us to harness our inner strength to achieve our potential.

- Day 3 Creation: The creation of vegetation represents the initiation of growth and the vitality of the earth. The Solar Plexus Chakra, similarly, embodies the drive for personal growth and the energy needed to manifest our ambitions.

3. Connection to Nature

- Solar Plexus Chakra: This chakra fosters our connection to the natural world and our environment, influencing our relationship with the physical aspects of life.

- Day 3 Creation: The introduction of plants and trees not only signifies the beauty of creation but also our interconnectedness with nature. The Solar Plexus Chakra encourages us to appreciate and engage with the natural world, reinforcing our sense of place and purpose.

4. Manifestation and Action

- Solar Plexus Chakra: Associated with the act of manifestation, this chakra inspires us to take decisive actions toward our goals and dreams.

- Day 3 Creation: The command to let the earth bring forth vegetation represents the act of manifestation itself. It reflects the idea that through focused intention and action, we can create and nurture life, similar to how the Solar Plexus Chakra propels us to turn our ideas into reality.

5. Identity and Self-Expression

- Solar Plexus Chakra: This chakra is closely linked to our sense of self and how we express our individuality.

- Day 3 Creation: The differentiation of land and the introduction of diverse plant life signify the uniqueness and variety within creation. The Solar Plexus Chakra encourages us to embrace our individuality and express ourselves confidently in the world, just as the diversity of plants and trees enriches the earth.

The Solar Plexus Chakra corresponds with Day 3 of Creation through its emphasis on personal power, growth, and the ability to manifest our desires. The gathering of waters to reveal dry land and the emergence of vegetation symbolize the foundation of life and the energy required to nurture it. This connection highlights the importance of harnessing our inner strength to create and grow, both in the physical world and within ourselves, encouraging a dynamic interplay between our personal development and our relationship with nature.

Day 3 Reincarnation

The third day of creation in Genesis details God's act of gathering the waters to reveal dry land and the emergence of plants and trees. This day can be correlated with the process of reincarnation in several profound ways:

1. Manifestation of Potential: The gathering of waters to reveal dry land symbolizes the idea of potential becoming reality. In reincarnation, the soul's journey involves moving from the spiritual realm—where it exists in potential—to a physical existence where it can manifest its lessons and growth. Just as dry land provides a foundation for life to thrive, the physical body serves as a vessel for the soul to express itself, learn, and evolve through various experiences.

2. Nurturing Environment: The creation of plants and trees on the third day represents the establishment of a nurturing environment essential for growth. Similarly, reincarnation provides the soul with various life experiences—each offering opportunities for growth and learning. The physical world, like the lushness of plants and trees, presents challenges and resources that aid the soul's development. Just as plants rely on the soil, sunlight, and water to flourish, the soul benefits from the diverse circumstances it encounters in each lifetime.

3. Interconnectedness of Life: The emergence of various forms of life on dry land signifies the interconnectedness of ecosystems. In reincarnation, the soul is not only influenced by its individual experiences but also by the relationships and interactions it has with others. Each life is interconnected, contributing to a larger tapestry of existence. This reflects the idea that the soul's journey is enriched by its interactions with other souls, much like how plants and trees rely on each other and their environment for survival.

4. Cycles of Renewal: The cyclical nature of growth in plants and trees parallels the cycle of reincarnation. Just as plants die and regenerate through seasons, the soul undergoes cycles of birth, death, and rebirth. Each incarnation provides the soul with a chance to learn from past experiences, evolve, and return to the cycle anew. This concept emphasizes the idea of renewal and the continuous opportunity for growth inherent in both the natural world and the spiritual journey.

5. Foundation for Life: The creation of dry land serves as the foundation for all terrestrial life. In the context of reincarnation, the body can be seen as the foundation upon which the soul's journey unfolds. It is through the physical body that the soul interacts with the material world, gaining insights and wisdom necessary for its evolution. Just as land is crucial for plant life to thrive, the physical form is essential for the soul's experiences and learning in each lifetime.

The third day of creation, with its focus on dry land, seas, and the flourishing of plants and trees, serves as a powerful analogy for the process of reincarnation. It illustrates themes of potential realization, the nurturing environment for growth, the interconnectedness of life, cycles of renewal, and the foundational role of the physical body. Both processes emphasize the importance of learning, growth, and the continuous journey of the soul through various incarnations.

Day 3 Nuanced

Solar Plexus Chakra (Manipura): A Nuanced Perspective in Relation to Creation and Reincarnation

The Solar Plexus Chakra, or Manipura, is the third energy center in the chakra system, representing personal power, confidence, and will. It governs our sense of self, our drive for achievement, and our ability to take action. In the context of the creation story and the process of reincarnation, the Solar Plexus Chakra embodies themes of individuality, purpose, and the transformative power of personal will. Here's a nuanced exploration of its significance:

1. The Birth of Individuality

- Creation as an Expression of Will: The creation narrative illustrates God's will manifesting as the cosmos comes into existence. Each element, from light to living creatures, reflects a unique aspect of divine intention. Similarly, the Solar Plexus Chakra represents our own individuality and the assertion of personal power. In the reincarnation process, each soul is imbued with a distinct purpose and a mission to fulfill in the physical realm, mirroring the uniqueness of each creation in the biblical account.

2. Empowerment and Purpose

- Finding One's Path: The Solar Plexus Chakra empowers us to discover our life purpose. Just as the creation story unfolds with intentional design, our reincarnation journey is about embracing our mission and exercising our free will. The manipulation of energy in the Solar Plexus Chakra encourages us to take responsibility for our choices and recognize the impact of our actions on our spiritual evolution. This empowerment is essential for navigating the lessons and challenges that arise during our earthly experiences.

3. Confidence in Manifestation

- From Intention to Reality: The act of creation involves not just the intention but also the power to manifest that intention into reality. The Solar Plexus Chakra serves as a conduit for this energy, channeling our desires and ambitions into tangible outcomes. In the reincarnation process, this chakra allows us to take decisive action towards our goals and to manifest our spiritual lessons into practical life experiences. Embracing the energy of the Solar Plexus enables us to create the life we envision for ourselves.

4. Transformative Challenges

- Growth Through Struggle: The creation story illustrates the complexity of existence, filled with challenges and opportunities for growth. The Solar Plexus Chakra reminds us that personal power is often forged in the fires of adversity. In reincarnation, we encounter obstacles designed to strengthen our resolve and help us develop resilience. By facing these challenges with confidence, we harness the transformative energy of the Solar Plexus to emerge stronger and more aligned with our true selves.

5. Balancing Will and Surrender

- The Dance of Control and Acceptance: While the Solar Plexus Chakra emphasizes personal power, it also highlights the importance of balancing that power with surrender. In the creation narrative, God's will is ultimately supreme, reflecting a divine order that transcends individual desires. In reincarnation, this balance is crucial; while we must assert our will to shape our destiny, we also need to recognize the larger forces at play. The Solar Plexus teaches us to harness our will while remaining open to the lessons and guidance that life presents.

6. Connection to Others

- Interpersonal Dynamics of Power: The Solar Plexus Chakra is not just about individual empowerment; it also relates to our interactions with others. Just as the creation of life involves relationships and ecosystems, the Solar Plexus reflects how we assert our personal power in social dynamics. In the reincarnation process, our relationships influence our development and provide contexts in which we learn about power, dominance, and collaboration. Understanding these dynamics enhances our ability to navigate social landscapes effectively.

7. Emotional Regulation and Stability

- Harnessing Emotions for Action: The Solar Plexus Chakra plays a crucial role in emotional regulation, which is vital for manifesting intentions. In the creation story, the emotional undertones of creation reflect the complexity of life. Similarly, the reincarnation journey requires us to navigate a spectrum of emotions, and the Solar Plexus helps us harness these feelings constructively. By cultivating emotional stability, we can channel our passions and desires into purposeful action.

8. The Role of Personal Responsibility

- Ownership of Choices: The Solar Plexus Chakra emphasizes personal responsibility for one's life choices. In the context of creation, each act of divine creation bears the weight of intention and consequence. In reincarnation, recognizing that our choices shape our experiences is essential for growth. By taking ownership of our actions and their outcomes, we align ourselves with the purpose of our soul's journey, allowing for deeper learning and transformation.

The Solar Plexus Chakra offers profound insights into the connections between the creation story and the process of reincarnation. By embodying personal power, purpose, and responsibility, we navigate our journeys with intention and clarity. The themes of individuality, empowerment, and transformation resonate throughout the creation narrative, reminding us that our lives are both unique expressions of divine will and opportunities for profound growth. As we harness the energy of the Solar Plexus Chakra, we embrace our role as co-creators in the unfolding tapestry of existence, using our will to shape our destinies while remaining open to the lessons life has to offer.

Day 4: Correlation between day 4 creation and the experience of the soul in the womb

The fourth day of creation, where God establishes the Sun, Moon, and stars to govern day and night and provide light for the earth, can be correlated with the experience of the soul in the womb in several insightful ways:

1. Illumination and Awareness: The creation of light sources on the fourth day symbolizes the emergence of awareness and understanding. Similarly, within the womb, as the fetus develops, the soul begins to experience a heightened sense of awareness. This growing consciousness parallels the way the Sun and Moon illuminate the world, allowing for clarity and comprehension.

2. Cycles and Rhythms: The establishment of day and night signifies the introduction of cycles and natural rhythms. In the womb, the soul is also influenced by biological rhythms, such as the mother's heartbeat and daily cycles. These rhythms create a sense of stability and predictability, mirroring the cosmic cycles established by the heavenly bodies.

3. Guidance and Direction: The Sun, Moon, and stars serve as guides for navigation and understanding one's place in the universe. In a similar way, the soul in the womb begins to develop its own sense of direction and purpose. This phase is crucial as the soul starts to align itself with the energies and influences that will shape its life after birth.

4. Connection to the Universe: The celestial bodies represent a connection to the greater universe. As the soul grows in the womb, it begins to form a sense of belonging not just to its immediate environment but to the vastness of existence. This connection fosters a deeper understanding of its role within the cosmos.

5. Duality and Balance: The Sun and Moon symbolize duality—light and dark, masculine and feminine. Within the womb, the soul is surrounded by the duality of experiences as it prepares for life. This duality can represent the balance of emotions, energies, and influences that the soul will encounter in its earthly journey.

6. Transformation and Growth: The fourth day signifies transformation as light transforms the earth. Similarly, the womb is a space of transformation for the soul, where it evolves from a simple embryo to a fully formed being. This

transformation is essential for the soul to fully inhabit its physical form and express its unique identity.

7. Hope and Potential: The Sun rising each day represents hope and new beginnings. In the womb, the soul experiences the potential for life and growth. This sense of hope is vital, as it fuels the soul's anticipation of the experiences and opportunities that lie ahead.

8. Orientation and Perspective: The stars provide a framework for orientation and perspective, guiding travelers and seekers. As the soul develops in the womb, it begins to form a perspective on existence, learning to navigate its internal and external worlds. This orientation is crucial for understanding relationships and interactions after birth.

The correlation between the fourth day of creation and the experience of the soul in the womb highlights themes of illumination, cycles, guidance, and transformation. Both processes reflect the importance of awareness and understanding, as the soul prepares to enter a world filled with opportunities and challenges. Just as the celestial bodies illuminate the path for life on earth, the womb serves as a sacred space for the soul to grow, develop, and ultimately emerge into the light of existence.

Day 4 Chakra

The energy chakra that corresponds to Day 4 of Creation, when God created the Sun, Moon, and stars to govern day and night, is the Heart Chakra (Anahata). Here's how they relate:

1. Love and Compassion

- Heart Chakra: This chakra embodies love, compassion, and emotional connection. It governs our ability to give and receive love, fostering empathy and kindness.

- Day 4 Creation: The creation of celestial bodies represents the nurturing cycles of day and night, reminding us of the importance of connection and harmony in our relationships. The Heart Chakra enables us to cultivate love for ourselves and others, just as the celestial bodies reflect the rhythms of life.

2. Balance and Harmony

- Heart Chakra: This chakra promotes balance in our emotional states and relationships, encouraging us to harmonize our feelings and connections.

- Day 4 Creation: The establishment of day and night symbolizes the duality of existence—light and dark, joy and sorrow. This balance mirrors the Heart Chakra's role in helping us navigate our emotional landscape, integrating our experiences for greater harmony.

3. Unity and Connection

- Heart Chakra: The Heart Chakra is central to our sense of connection to others and the universe. It fosters a feeling of unity and belonging.

- Day 4 Creation: The stars invite contemplation of our place in the cosmos, reminding us that we are part of a larger whole. The Heart Chakra encourages us to embrace this interconnectedness, nurturing our relationships and our bond with the universe.

4. Healing and Transformation

- Heart Chakra: This chakra is essential for emotional healing and personal transformation, allowing us to release pain and open to love.

- Day 4 Creation: The Sun provides light and warmth, symbolizing growth and renewal. This illumination reflects the Heart Chakra's power to heal and transform our emotional landscape, enabling us to move forward with love and purpose.

5. Joy and Gratitude

- Heart Chakra: Associated with joy and gratitude, the Heart Chakra invites us to appreciate life's beauty and express our happiness.

- Day 4 Creation: The celestial bodies inspire awe and wonder, encouraging us to celebrate the natural world. The Heart Chakra enhances our ability to experience joy and gratitude, reminding us to embrace the beauty around us.

The Heart Chakra aligns with Day 4 of Creation through its emphasis on love, compassion, and emotional connection. The creation of the Sun, Moon, and stars not only illuminates the physical world but also serves as a metaphor for the nurturing of our hearts and relationships. This connection highlights the importance of fostering love and unity, embracing the balance of light and dark, and cultivating gratitude for our journey. By nurturing our Heart Chakra, we can enhance our emotional well-being and navigate our lives with love and intention.

Day 4 Reincarnation

The fourth day of creation in Genesis describes God creating the Sun, Moon, and stars, establishing a celestial framework that governs time and seasons. This day can be correlated with the process of reincarnation in several meaningful ways:

1. Illumination and Guidance: The Sun, as a source of light, symbolizes illumination and guidance in our lives. In the context of reincarnation, this can represent the soul's journey toward enlightenment. Just as the Sun provides the necessary light for life on Earth, spiritual teachings and experiences illuminate the path for the soul, guiding it through its various incarnations. The light can be seen as the wisdom gained through each lifetime, helping the soul navigate its journey more effectively.

2. Cycles and Rhythms: The creation of the Moon and stars introduces the idea of cycles, rhythms, and the passage of time. Similarly, reincarnation operates within cycles of life, death, and rebirth. The Moon's phases reflect the cyclical nature of existence, where the soul experiences different stages in its journey. Each lifetime can be viewed as a phase, contributing to the overall growth and evolution of the soul, just as each lunar phase plays a role in the natural world.

3. Separation of Light and Darkness: On the fourth day, God distinguishes between day and night, symbolizing the duality of existence. This can relate to the soul's journey through reincarnation, where experiences can be seen as oscillating between light (growth, knowledge) and darkness (ignorance, challenges). The contrasts between light and dark in life serve as opportunities for the soul to learn and evolve, much like how the night allows for reflection and rest before the dawn of new insights and experiences.

4. Cosmic Connection: The stars represent the vastness of the universe and the interconnectedness of all things. In reincarnation, the soul is part of a larger cosmic design, indicating that each individual journey is interconnected with others. Just as the stars are part of a grand tapestry, each soul contributes to the collective human experience, influencing and being influenced by others through various lifetimes.

5. Purpose and Direction: The Sun, Moon, and stars serve not only as light sources but also as markers for navigation. This aspect of creation can be correlated with the soul's purpose in each lifetime. Just as ancient navigators

used the stars to find their way, the soul uses the lessons learned and insights gained from previous lives to navigate its current incarnation. Understanding one's purpose helps the soul to grow and make choices that align with its higher path.

6. Reflection of the Inner Self: The Sun, Moon, and stars can also symbolize different aspects of the self. The Sun represents the conscious mind and outward expression, while the Moon embodies the subconscious and emotional world. The stars can symbolize the higher self or spiritual aspirations. In reincarnation, the soul continually strives to integrate these aspects, seeking balance and harmony within itself through various life experiences.

The fourth day of creation, marked by the formation of the Sun, Moon, and stars, serves as a profound analogy for the process of reincarnation. It illustrates themes of illumination, cycles of existence, the duality of light and darkness, cosmic interconnectedness, purpose and direction, and the reflection of the inner self. Together, these elements highlight the dynamic journey of the soul as it evolves through multiple lifetimes, guided by the wisdom of its experiences and the interconnectedness of all existence.

Day 4 Nuanced

Heart Chakra (Anahata): A Nuanced Perspective in Relation to Creation and Reincarnation

The Heart Chakra, or Anahata, is the fourth energy center in the chakra system, often associated with love, compassion, and emotional balance. It serves as a bridge between the lower chakras (which connect to our physical and survival needs) and the upper chakras (which relate to our spiritual and higher consciousness). In the context of the creation story and the process of reincarnation, the Heart Chakra embodies essential themes of connection, love, and the transformative power of compassion. Here are some nuanced perspectives on this relationship:

1. Divine Love as the Foundation of Creation

- Creation as an Act of Love: The creation story illustrates God's intention to create a world filled with life, beauty, and connection. This act can be viewed as a manifestation of divine love. Similarly, the Heart Chakra represents our ability to express and receive love. In the process of reincarnation, the energy of the Heart Chakra underscores the importance of love as a guiding force, reminding us that our soul's journey is rooted in love and connection to others.

2. Connection and Interconnectedness

- Web of Life: The Heart Chakra symbolizes the interconnectedness of all beings. Just as the creation story depicts a universe filled with diverse forms of life, the Heart Chakra invites us to recognize that our individual journeys are interwoven. In the context of reincarnation, this interconnectedness means that our actions and experiences impact not only our own lives but also the lives of others. The Heart Chakra encourages empathy and understanding, facilitating deeper connections with those around us.

3. Healing Through Compassion

- Transformative Power of Love: The Heart Chakra is closely associated with healing and compassion. In the creation narrative, the unfolding of life presents challenges and opportunities for growth. Similarly, the process of reincarnation often involves navigating emotional wounds and lessons. The Heart Chakra empowers us to approach these challenges with compassion—both for ourselves and for others. By embracing love as a healing force, we can transform our past experiences and foster growth in future incarnations.

4. Forgiveness and Release

- Letting Go of Past Burdens: The Heart Chakra plays a crucial role in the practice of forgiveness. In the context of the creation story, the act of creation invites us to release old patterns and embrace new beginnings. In reincarnation, we carry the lessons and experiences of previous lives, which may include unresolved emotions and attachments. By opening the Heart Chakra, we cultivate the ability to forgive ourselves and others, allowing us to let go of burdens and move forward with greater clarity and freedom.

5. Emotional Intelligence and Awareness

- Navigating Emotional Landscapes: The Heart Chakra encourages emotional intelligence and awareness. In the creation narrative, God's intentions reflect a deep understanding of the complexities of life. Similarly, the Heart Chakra invites us to become attuned to our own emotions and those of others. This awareness is essential during the reincarnation process, as it allows us to learn from our experiences and develop the emotional skills necessary for growth and connection in future lives.

6. The Role of Love in Spiritual Growth

- Guidance on the Path: The Heart Chakra serves as a guiding force on our spiritual journey. Love not only enriches our lives but also propels our spiritual evolution. In the creation story, the unfolding of life is imbued with purpose and meaning, reflecting the divine intention behind existence. In reincarnation, love acts as a compass, helping us navigate our path and learn the lessons necessary for our soul's growth. The Heart Chakra reminds us that the ultimate goal of our journey is to embody love in all its forms.

7. Nurturing Relationships

- The Importance of Connection: The Heart Chakra emphasizes the value of nurturing relationships. In the creation story, God creates not only the earth and its inhabitants but also the relationships that bind them together. In reincarnation, our connections with others are vital for our growth and healing. The Heart Chakra encourages us to cultivate love and compassion in our relationships, reminding us that these connections are essential to our spiritual journey.

8. Celebration of Life

- Embracing Joy and Gratitude: The Heart Chakra encourages us to celebrate life's experiences. Just as the creation story illustrates the beauty and diversity of existence, the Heart Chakra invites us to approach life with joy and gratitude. In the context of reincarnation, this perspective helps us embrace the lessons and opportunities each lifetime offers. By celebrating our experiences and the connections we forge, we align ourselves with the essence of love that the Heart Chakra embodies.

The Heart Chakra serves as a powerful lens through which to explore the connections between the creation story and the process of reincarnation. By embodying love, compassion, and interconnectedness, the Heart Chakra illuminates the spiritual journey of the soul. It encourages us to embrace our experiences, nurture our relationships, and navigate the complexities of life with emotional intelligence. Through the Heart Chakra, we come to understand that love is not only the foundation of creation but also the driving force behind our growth and evolution across lifetimes. Ultimately, the Heart Chakra invites us to celebrate the richness of existence and to recognize the divine purpose behind our journeys of reincarnation.

Day 5: Correlation between day 5 creation and the experience of the soul in the womb

The fifth day of creation, during which God creates the creatures of the sea and the birds of the air, provides a rich framework for understanding the experience of the soul in the womb. Here are several correlations:

1. Emergence of Life: The fifth day marks the flourishing of life forms—fish and birds—each thriving in their respective environments. Similarly, in the womb, the soul is surrounded by a nurturing environment, where it begins to develop and prepare for its own emergence into the world. This stage is crucial for the soul's growth and vitality.

2. Exploration and Freedom: The creatures of the sea and the skies represent freedom and exploration. In the womb, the soul experiences a sense of potential and exploration as it begins to sense the outside world. This awareness of possibility mirrors the instinctual drive of birds to fly and fish to swim, emphasizing the innate longing for freedom that will come to fruition after birth.

3. Diversity and Connection: The creation of diverse species highlights the beauty of life in all its forms. Within the womb, the soul develops an understanding of its unique identity while simultaneously recognizing its connection to the greater tapestry of existence. This reflects the idea that, while each creature is distinct, they all contribute to a larger ecosystem, much like individual souls contribute to the collective human experience.

4. Development of Sensory Awareness: The fifth day's emphasis on living creatures connects with the soul's developing sensory awareness in the womb. As the fetus grows, it begins to respond to sounds, movements, and other stimuli, mirroring the way aquatic and aerial creatures navigate their environments. This burgeoning awareness prepares the soul for interaction with the world outside.

5. Adaptation and Resilience: Sea creatures and birds exemplify adaptation to their environments. In the womb, the soul also learns to adapt to its surroundings, preparing for the various challenges it will face in life. This process of resilience is essential for the soul's growth, echoing the ability of creatures to thrive in diverse ecosystems.

6. Symbolism of Water and Air: Water, a vital element for sea life, symbolizes emotion and intuition, while air represents thought and inspiration. The womb,

filled with amniotic fluid, offers a nurturing, protective space where the soul can develop both emotionally and spiritually. This duality reflects the need for a balanced emotional and intellectual foundation for life.

7. Communal Existence: The interactions among sea creatures and birds emphasize community and interconnectedness. In the womb, the soul begins to sense its relationship with the mother and the environment, laying the groundwork for future social interactions and relationships. This early sense of connection is vital for the soul's journey into the world.

8. Preparation for Flight and Freedom: Birds are often seen as symbols of aspiration and freedom. The soul in the womb is similarly preparing for its own "flight" into life. This anticipation fosters a sense of hope and excitement, mirroring the instinctual drive in birds to take to the skies.

The correlation between the fifth day of creation and the experience of the soul in the womb underscores themes of life, exploration, adaptability, and interconnectedness. Both processes highlight the importance of growth in a nurturing environment, where the soul begins to sense its identity and potential, preparing for the journey ahead. Just as creatures of the sea and air thrive in their worlds, the soul in the womb is on the brink of a transformative journey into the greater expanse of life.

Day 5 Chakra

The energy chakra that corresponds to Day 5 of Creation, when God created the creatures of the sea and the birds of the air, is the Throat Chakra (Vishuddha). Here's how they relate:

1. Expression and Communication

- Throat Chakra: This chakra is primarily associated with communication, self-expression, and the ability to convey thoughts and emotions clearly.

- Day 5 Creation: The creation of sea creatures and birds symbolizes the diversity of life and the various ways beings communicate and express themselves. Just as different species have their unique calls and songs, the Throat Chakra encourages us to find our voice and express our true selves.

2. Creativity and Freedom

- Throat Chakra: Linked to creativity, the Throat Chakra allows us to articulate our ideas and express our individuality.

- Day 5 Creation: The freedom of birds to soar through the skies and the dynamic life of aquatic creatures reflect the essence of creativity and the limitless possibilities of expression. This aligns with the Throat Chakra's role in fostering creativity and the courage to share our unique perspectives.

3. Connection to Nature

- Throat Chakra: This chakra connects us to our environment, allowing us to communicate not only with others but also with nature.

- Day 5 Creation: The creation of creatures that inhabit the sea and sky invites us to appreciate and communicate with the natural world. The Throat Chakra facilitates our understanding of nature's rhythms and the interconnectedness of all living beings.

4. Listening and Understanding

- Throat Chakra: Effective communication is not just about speaking; it also involves active listening and understanding others.

- Day 5 Creation: In the context of creatures that communicate through sounds, Day 5 emphasizes the importance of listening to the messages of the natural world. The Throat Chakra encourages us to cultivate this ability to listen, enhancing our relationships with both people and nature.

5. Symbol of Diversity

- Throat Chakra: This chakra represents the unique voices and expressions of individuals, celebrating diversity in communication and creativity.

- Day 5 Creation: The variety of creatures created on this day exemplifies the beauty of diversity in nature. Each species has its unique way of contributing to the ecosystem, much like how each person's voice adds richness to human interaction. The Throat Chakra fosters an appreciation for this diversity and encourages respectful dialogue.

The Throat Chakra aligns with Day 5 of Creation through its emphasis on communication, expression, and creativity. The creation of sea creatures and birds serves as a reminder of the importance of finding our voice and connecting with the world around us. By nurturing our Throat Chakra, we can enhance our ability to communicate authentically, embrace our creative potential, and deepen our connections with both nature and humanity. This alignment highlights the significance of self-expression in fostering understanding and harmony in our lives.

Day 5 Reincarnation

The fifth day of creation in Genesis describes God creating creatures that inhabit the sea and those that fly in the air. This day can be correlated with the process of reincarnation in several insightful ways:

1. Diversity of Existence: The creation of various sea creatures and birds highlights the diversity of life and experiences. Similarly, reincarnation encompasses a wide array of lifetimes, allowing the soul to explore different forms, identities, and circumstances. Just as the ocean is home to countless species, each with unique adaptations, the journey of reincarnation provides the soul with diverse experiences to learn and grow from.

2. Freedom and Exploration: Birds symbolize freedom, the ability to soar above earthly concerns, and the exploration of new perspectives. In the context of reincarnation, this reflects the soul's desire for growth and expansion. Each new life offers opportunities to rise above past limitations, to gain new insights, and to transcend previous experiences. This notion of freedom resonates with the idea that the soul is not bound to a single path but is encouraged to explore the vastness of existence.

3. Depth of Experience: The creatures of the sea inhabit a realm that is often seen as mysterious and profound. This can symbolize the depths of the subconscious and the emotional experiences that the soul navigates throughout its many incarnations. Just as the ocean is a place of both beauty and darkness, reincarnation allows the soul to dive into the depths of experience, facing challenges and discovering treasures of wisdom that lie beneath the surface.

4. Adaptation and Survival: Sea creatures and flying creatures have adapted to their environments, showcasing the importance of flexibility and resilience. In reincarnation, the soul must also adapt to new circumstances in each lifetime, learning to navigate different challenges and environments. This theme emphasizes growth through adaptability, as the soul learns to thrive in varying situations and emerges stronger and wiser with each incarnation.

5. Symbolism of Water and Air: Water often represents emotions, intuition, and the subconscious, while air symbolizes intellect, communication, and the spirit. The creation of sea creatures and birds can be seen as a balance between these elements. In reincarnation, the soul must navigate both emotional and

intellectual realms, integrating feelings and thoughts to achieve a harmonious existence. This duality allows for a fuller understanding of the self and enhances spiritual development.

6. Interconnectedness of Life: Both sea and flying creatures play crucial roles in their ecosystems, highlighting the interconnectedness of all living beings. Similarly, the process of reincarnation emphasizes that individual souls are part of a larger tapestry of existence. Each life affects others, creating a web of relationships and influences that shape the collective experience. Understanding this interconnectedness fosters compassion and empathy, essential qualities for personal and spiritual growth.

7. Cycles of Life: The rhythmic patterns of life in both aquatic and aerial environments reflect the cyclical nature of existence. Reincarnation operates within these cycles, where the soul experiences birth, death, and rebirth. The movements of creatures in their respective environments can symbolize the ebb and flow of life experiences, reminding us that each phase, whether joyful or challenging, contributes to the soul's journey.

The fifth day of creation, marked by the emergence of sea creatures and birds, serves as a rich analogy for the process of reincarnation. It emphasizes diversity of existence, freedom of exploration, depth of experience, adaptability, the interplay of emotions and intellect, interconnectedness, and the cyclical nature of life. Together, these themes underscore the dynamic journey of the soul as it evolves through multiple lifetimes, continually seeking growth, understanding, and connection within the vast universe of existence.

Day 5 Nuanced

Throat Chakra (Vishuddha): A Nuanced Perspective in Relation to Creation and Reincarnation

The Throat Chakra, or Vishuddha, is the fifth energy center in the chakra system and is primarily associated with communication, expression, and truth. In the context of the creation story and reincarnation, this chakra holds significant implications for how we articulate our experiences, convey our truths, and connect with the divine. Here are some nuanced perspectives on the Throat Chakra as it relates to both the creation narrative and the journey of the soul through reincarnation:

1. Communication as Creation

- Words as Creative Forces: In the creation story, the act of God speaking the world into existence underscores the profound power of words. Similarly, the Throat Chakra symbolizes the energy of communication that shapes our reality. Each utterance carries the potential to create, heal, or destroy. Understanding this connection encourages us to be mindful of our words, recognizing that our expressions can manifest realities not only for ourselves but also for those around us.

2. Authentic Self-Expression

- Voicing the Soul's Truth: Just as God spoke creation into being, individuals are called to express their authentic selves. This aligns with the process of reincarnation, where the soul returns to embody its lessons and truths. The Throat Chakra invites us to communicate our innermost thoughts and feelings, fostering authenticity. When we suppress our voices, we hinder the soul's growth, preventing it from fully realizing its purpose in each life.

3. Healing Through Expression

- Cleansing Past Wounds: The Throat Chakra serves as a conduit for healing, allowing us to express unspoken emotions and experiences. In the context of reincarnation, many souls carry unresolved issues from previous lives. By vocalizing these feelings and experiences, we can initiate healing and closure. Therapeutic practices such as journaling, singing, or participating in group discussions can facilitate this release, enabling the soul to transcend past pain and embrace new beginnings.

4. Listening as a Form of Communication

- The Art of Active Listening: Effective communication is not solely about speaking; it also involves listening. The Throat Chakra teaches us the importance of hearing others' truths. In relationships and communities, active listening fosters deeper connections and understanding. This practice allows us to honor the experiences of others, creating a supportive environment where healing and growth can occur.

5. The Role of Intention

- Conscious Communication: The Throat Chakra emphasizes that the intention behind our words is as vital as the words themselves. When communicating our truths, we must be conscious of our intentions—are we seeking to uplift, inform, or manipulate? This self-awareness shapes the outcome of our interactions and influences the collective energy within our communities. Intentional communication can transform conflicts into opportunities for understanding and growth.

6. Expressing Spiritual Experiences

- Articulating the Inexpressible: Many spiritual experiences—especially those related to reincarnation—can be difficult to articulate. The Throat Chakra provides the energy needed to express these profound realizations. Whether through storytelling, poetry, or art, sharing our spiritual journeys allows others to resonate with our experiences, fostering a sense of community and shared understanding.

7. Balancing Personal and Collective Narratives

- Creating Shared Realities: The Throat Chakra also highlights the balance between personal and collective narratives. In the creation story, God's voice shaped the cosmos, a reminder of how individual expressions contribute to the larger tapestry of existence. Each person's truth adds to the collective consciousness. By recognizing our roles in shaping communal realities, we can engage in dialogues that uplift and empower others.

8. Reincarnation as an Ongoing Dialogue

- The Continuous Cycle of Expression: The journey of reincarnation can be viewed as an ongoing dialogue between the soul and the universe. Each life presents an opportunity to refine our expressions, learn new lessons, and evolve. The Throat Chakra facilitates this continuous process, encouraging us to articulate our experiences and insights, thus enhancing our spiritual growth.

The Throat Chakra represents the power of expression, communication, and truth within the context of creation and reincarnation. By nurturing this energy center, we honor our voices and the voices of others, fostering an environment where healing, authenticity, and connection can flourish. As we recognize the profound impact of our words and intentions, we empower ourselves and those around us to engage in a deeper dialogue with life, ultimately contributing to the spiritual evolution of all beings. The Throat Chakra reminds us that through conscious communication, we can create and shape our realities, both individually and collectively, echoing the divine act of creation itself.

Day 6: Correlation between day 6 creation and the experience of the soul in the womb

The sixth day of creation, which focuses on the creation of land animals and humanity, offers profound correlations with the experience of the soul in the womb. Here are several key points that illustrate this connection:

1. Formation of Identity: On the sixth day, God creates animals and humans, emphasizing individuality and the distinct qualities of each creation. In the womb, the soul begins to develop a sense of identity. This process involves recognizing its unique essence, much like how each animal embodies specific traits and characteristics. The nurturing environment of the womb allows the soul to contemplate its individuality and role within the larger framework of existence.

2. Connection to the Physical World: The creation of land animals symbolizes the soul's eventual connection to the physical realm. As the fetus develops, it becomes more attuned to physical sensations and experiences, such as touch and movement. This connection to the physical body is essential for the soul's journey, as it prepares for life outside the womb, much like the animals created on this day that interact with their environments.

3. Relationships and Community: The sixth day highlights the importance of relationships, particularly with the creation of humans who are made in the image of God. In the womb, the soul begins forming a bond with the mother, laying the groundwork for future relationships. This early attachment is crucial for emotional development and reflects the interconnectedness seen in both human and animal communities.

4. Purpose and Responsibility: The creation of humans includes the divine directive to have dominion over the earth. This reflects a sense of purpose and responsibility. In the womb, the soul is gradually preparing to fulfill its own purpose in life. The awareness of this potential encourages the soul to embrace its future role, mirroring the way humans are entrusted with stewardship of creation.

5. Development of Emotions and Consciousness: As land animals and humans are created, there is an emphasis on the development of consciousness and emotional capacity. In the womb, the soul begins to experience emotions,

responding to the mother's feelings and the external environment. This emotional awareness lays the foundation for complex interactions and relationships after birth.

6. The Gift of Life: The sixth day culminates in the creation of human beings, emphasizing the sacredness of life. In the womb, the soul is surrounded by the miracle of development—growing, thriving, and preparing for birth. This profound experience mirrors the divine act of creation, as both the soul and the body evolve together in a sacred process.

7. Physical Preparation: As animals are created to inhabit the land, the fetus is physically prepared for life in the world. This includes developing the senses, bodily functions, and physical attributes necessary for survival. The physical growth in the womb corresponds with the diverse forms of life created on the sixth day, each adapted to its environment.

8. Unity of Spirit and Body: The creation of humans in the image of God signifies a unique union of spirit and body. In the womb, the soul and body are intricately connected, forming a holistic entity. This connection emphasizes the importance of recognizing the body as a vessel for the soul's experiences and growth.

The sixth day of creation and the experience of the soul in the womb are intricately linked through themes of identity, connection, purpose, and the sacredness of life. Both processes underscore the importance of emotional and physical development, the nurturing of relationships, and the preparation for the soul's journey in the world. The creation narrative enriches our understanding of the profound journey from the womb to life, highlighting the divine purpose inherent in each soul's existence.

Day 6 Chakra

The energy chakra that corresponds to Day 6 of Creation, when God created land animals and humans, is the Third Eye Chakra (Ajna). Here's how they relate:

1. Intuition and Insight

- Third Eye Chakra: The Third Eye Chakra is associated with intuition, insight, and the ability to see beyond the surface. It allows us to access deeper understanding and clarity.

- Day 6 Creation: The creation of land animals and humans emphasizes the evolution of consciousness and awareness. Just as the Third Eye Chakra enhances our perceptive abilities, this day symbolizes the awakening of human understanding and the role of animals in enriching our lives.

2. Perception of Self and Others

- Third Eye Chakra: This chakra influences how we perceive ourselves and the world, shaping our thoughts and beliefs.

- Day 6 Creation: The creation of humans, made in God's image, underscores the importance of self-awareness and reflection. It highlights our capacity for empathy and understanding, which are vital for meaningful relationships with others and the environment.

3. Vision and Purpose

- Third Eye Chakra: The Third Eye Chakra helps us set intentions and visualize our goals, guiding our life direction.

- Day 6 Creation: The introduction of humans into creation brings forth a unique purpose and the ability to envision a future. This mirrors the Third Eye's function of helping us understand our individual and collective paths.

4. Integration of Intellect and Instinct

- Third Eye Chakra: This chakra promotes the balance of rational thought and intuitive wisdom.

- Day 6 Creation: The creation of animals represents instinctual knowledge, while humans embody a blend of intellect and intuition. The Third Eye Chakra aids in harmonizing these aspects, allowing us to navigate life with both reason and gut feelings.

5. Connection to the Universe

- Third Eye Chakra: The Third Eye connects us to higher consciousness and spiritual truths, expanding our awareness beyond the physical.

- Day 6 Creation: The relationship between humans and animals reflects our interconnectedness with all life forms and the universe. This connection invites us to explore deeper truths about our existence and our responsibilities within the ecological system.

The Third Eye Chakra aligns with Day 6 of Creation through its focus on insight, awareness, and our connection to the larger world. The creation of land animals and humans represents the importance of developing our intuition and understanding our place within the intricate web of life. By nurturing our Third Eye Chakra, we can enhance our perception, foster self-awareness, and navigate our journey with clarity and purpose. This alignment underscores the significance of recognizing our roles as conscious beings, embracing both our instincts and insights in caring for the earth and its inhabitants.

Day 6 Reincarnation

The sixth day of creation in Genesis is marked by the formation of land animals and the creation of humans in the image of God. This day can be correlated with the process of reincarnation in several meaningful ways:

1. Diversity of Life Forms: The creation of various land animals reflects the richness and diversity of life on Earth. In the context of reincarnation, this mirrors the multitude of experiences that souls undergo through different lifetimes. Just as land animals possess distinct traits and adaptations, each reincarnation allows the soul to inhabit a unique form, contributing to its overall development and understanding of existence.

2. The Image of God: Humans being created in the image of God signifies a unique connection to the divine and an inherent potential for spiritual growth. This parallels the reincarnation process, where each lifetime presents an opportunity for the soul to evolve and embody higher qualities. The idea of being made in the image of God emphasizes the soul's capacity for creativity, compassion, and moral understanding, traits that are nurtured and refined through various lifetimes.

3. Responsibility and Stewardship: With the creation of animals, humans are called to be stewards of the Earth. This responsibility can be seen as an extension of the soul's journey in reincarnation, where lessons in empathy, respect, and caretaking for other beings are paramount. Each incarnation offers opportunities to learn about interconnectedness and the impact of one's actions, fostering a sense of responsibility towards the world and its inhabitants.

4. Moral and Ethical Growth: The sixth day underscores the importance of moral decision-making, especially in the relationship between humans and animals. In reincarnation, the soul confronts various moral dilemmas, allowing for ethical growth. Each lifetime is a chance to refine one's understanding of right and wrong, cultivating virtues such as kindness, justice, and compassion, which are essential for spiritual evolution.

5. Interconnectedness of Life: The creation of land animals and humans highlights the interconnected web of life. Just as all creatures play a role in the ecosystem, reincarnation emphasizes that all souls are part of a larger spiritual network. This interconnectedness fosters a sense of unity and compassion,

encouraging individuals to recognize their shared humanity and the common threads that bind all life.

6. Physical and Spiritual Evolution: The progression from land animals to humans symbolizes a journey towards greater consciousness and self-awareness. In reincarnation, the soul evolves through various forms, moving from instinctual existence to a more conscious experience. This process allows the soul to gain insights into its true nature, ultimately striving for higher spiritual awareness and connection with the divine.

7. Challenges and Lessons: The sixth day introduces the complexities of life on land, including challenges faced by both animals and humans. Similarly, reincarnation presents the soul with challenges that serve as lessons for growth. Each lifetime offers opportunities to confront fears, overcome obstacles, and learn from experiences, facilitating spiritual development and resilience.

8. The Cycle of Birth and Death: The creation narrative emphasizes the cycle of life through the birth of land animals and humans. This parallels the cycle of reincarnation, where birth, death, and rebirth are integral aspects of the soul's journey. Understanding this cycle encourages acceptance of the natural flow of life, fostering a deeper appreciation for each experience.

The sixth day of creation, which encompasses the formation of land animals and the creation of humans in the image of God, serves as a profound analogy for the process of reincarnation. It highlights the diversity of life, the divine potential within humanity, the responsibility of stewardship, moral growth, interconnectedness, evolution, challenges, and the cyclical nature of existence. Together, these themes illustrate the dynamic journey of the soul as it navigates through multiple lifetimes, continually seeking understanding, growth, and a deeper connection to the divine and the world around it.

Day 6 Nuanced

Third Eye Chakra (Ajna): A Nuanced Perspective in Relation to Creation and Reincarnation

The Third Eye Chakra, or Ajna, is the sixth energy center in the chakra system, associated with intuition, perception, and the ability to see beyond the physical realm. It plays a pivotal role in how we interpret our experiences and understand the deeper truths of existence. In the context of the creation story and the process of reincarnation, the Third Eye Chakra embodies a profound connection between spiritual insight and the evolution of the soul. Here are some nuanced perspectives on this relationship:

1. Intuition as a Source of Creation

- Vision Beyond the Physical: In the creation narrative, God's vision precedes the act of creation, suggesting that all physical manifestations originate from a higher understanding or divine blueprint. The Third Eye Chakra enhances our intuition, enabling us to access this inner vision. Just as creation unfolds through divine intention, our insights can guide us in manifesting our realities. Tapping into this intuition allows us to align our actions with our true purpose.

2. Perception of Interconnectedness

- Seeing the Bigger Picture: The Third Eye Chakra fosters a sense of interconnectedness among all beings. In the context of reincarnation, this perspective helps us recognize that every soul's journey is part of a larger tapestry. Understanding that our lives are intertwined encourages compassion and empathy towards others, as we begin to see them not just as separate entities but as part of a collective journey towards growth and enlightenment.

3. Awakening Spiritual Sight

- Beyond the Veil of Illusion: The Third Eye Chakra invites us to pierce through the illusions of the material world, much like the divine vision that guided creation. This ability to "see" beyond physical appearances allows us to understand the deeper motivations and lessons behind our reincarnational experiences. By awakening our spiritual sight, we can discern the patterns and lessons that transcend individual lifetimes, facilitating a deeper understanding of our soul's purpose.

4. Integration of Past Experiences

- Viewing Past Lives: The Third Eye Chakra enables us to access memories and lessons from past lives, facilitating healing and integration. Just as the creation story outlines the stages of forming the universe, our own spiritual evolution requires us to synthesize experiences from our previous incarnations. This integration helps us recognize recurring themes and unresolved issues, allowing us to approach our current life with greater wisdom.

5. Clarity in Decision-Making

- Guided Choices: The intuitive clarity provided by the Third Eye Chakra empowers us to make choices aligned with our highest good. In the context of reincarnation, this clarity can guide us in navigating the challenges and opportunities presented in our current life. By honing our intuition, we can better discern our true path, avoiding decisions driven by fear or illusion.

6. Expanding Consciousness

- A Portal to Higher Realms: The Third Eye Chakra serves as a gateway to higher states of consciousness, enabling us to explore spiritual dimensions beyond the physical. This aligns with the creation story's theme of manifesting higher truths into the physical realm. By expanding our consciousness, we can engage with spiritual wisdom and insight, deepening our understanding of the cycles of life, death, and rebirth.

7. Illumination of Inner Truths

- Illuminating Self-Knowledge: Just as the creation of light brought clarity to the universe, the Third Eye Chakra illuminates our inner truths. This illumination fosters self-awareness, helping us confront and embrace our authentic selves. Understanding our true nature is crucial in the reincarnation process, as it empowers us to learn from our experiences and evolve spiritually.

8. Manifesting Intentions

- The Role of Visualization: The Third Eye Chakra also emphasizes the power of visualization in the creative process. By consciously visualizing our intentions and desired outcomes, we can manifest our realities more effectively. This practice aligns with the divine act of creation, where intention precedes manifestation. In the context of reincarnation, visualizing our goals and aspirations can guide our soul's journey, helping us stay focused on our purpose.

The Third Eye Chakra serves as a vital link between the creation story and the reincarnational journey, illuminating the interplay of intuition, perception, and spiritual insight. By nurturing this energy center, we enhance our ability to see beyond the surface of our experiences, fostering a deeper understanding of our place in the universe. The Third Eye invites us to embrace our spiritual vision, recognize our interconnectedness, and integrate the lessons of our past, ultimately guiding us toward greater self-awareness and purposeful living. Through the lens of the Third Eye, we can navigate the complexities of life with clarity and wisdom, echoing the divine principles that underpin both creation and reincarnation.

Day 7: Correlation between day 7 creation and the experience of the soul in the womb

The seventh day of creation, when God rests and sanctifies the day, can be richly correlated with the experience of the soul in the womb. This correlation emphasizes themes of completion, sacredness, and the transition to new beginnings. Here are several key points illustrating this connection:

1. Completion and Fulfillment: On the seventh day, God declares His creation "very good" and rests, marking the completion of His work. Similarly, the experience of the soul in the womb is one of completion as it nears the end of its gestation period. The soul is prepared to emerge into the world, fulfilling its purpose and potential. This period of rest in the womb mirrors the divine rest, symbolizing a time of reflection and anticipation before entering a new phase of existence.

2. Sacredness of Life: The sanctification of the seventh day highlights the holiness of creation. In the womb, the soul experiences a sacred environment where it is nurtured and protected. This sense of sacredness is vital for the soul's development, instilling an understanding of its inherent value and purpose. The womb becomes a hallowed space, akin to the sanctity of the seventh day.

3. Spiritual Preparation: The act of resting suggests a time of spiritual preparation and contemplation. In the womb, the soul is not only developing physically but is also undergoing a spiritual journey. It may be gathering wisdom and understanding, preparing to engage with the world beyond the womb. This preparation aligns with the idea of resting and reflecting on the journey ahead.

4. Transition and New Beginnings: The seventh day signifies a pause before the beginning of human life outside the womb. As the soul prepares for birth, it is on the cusp of a significant transition. This day represents a moment of stillness and readiness, allowing the soul to gather strength for the challenges and experiences that await. It embodies the idea of preparing for a new chapter in existence.

5. Connection to Divine Purpose: Just as God's rest symbolizes a completion of divine purpose, the soul's time in the womb is about fulfilling its own unique purpose. The nurturing environment allows the soul to understand its role in the larger tapestry of life. This sense of purpose reinforces the idea that the soul is

entering the world not just to exist, but to contribute meaningfully to the greater good.

6. Unity and Harmony: The seventh day reflects a state of harmony in creation. In the womb, the soul experiences a harmonious relationship with the mother, who provides the essential support and nourishment needed for growth. This unity fosters a sense of belonging and connection, which is crucial for the soul's emotional and spiritual development.

7. Rest and Reflection: The concept of rest is not just physical but also emotional and spiritual. The womb serves as a sanctuary where the soul can rest before the demands of the external world begin. This period allows for reflection on its journey and the life it is about to enter, paralleling God's rest on the seventh day.

8. Celebration of Life: The seventh day can be seen as a celebration of all that has been created. Similarly, the culmination of the womb experience is a celebration of life—the anticipation of birth, the joy of new beginnings, and the promise of the future. This celebration acknowledges the profound significance of the soul's journey from the spirit realm into the physical world.

The seventh day of creation and the experience of the soul in the womb are interconnected through themes of completion, sacredness, and preparation for new beginnings. Both emphasize the importance of reflection, unity, and the divine purpose inherent in life. This correlation enriches our understanding of the profound journey of the soul, highlighting the sacredness of its transition from the womb to the world.

Day 7 Chakra

The energy chakra that best corresponds to Day 7 of Creation, when God finished His work and rested, is the Crown Chakra (Sahasrara). Here's how they relate:

1. Completion and Fulfillment

- Crown Chakra: The Crown Chakra represents a sense of completion, spiritual enlightenment, and connection to the divine. It embodies the pinnacle of consciousness and awareness.

- Day 7 Creation: On this day, God completed the creation process, symbolizing fulfillment and the achievement of a greater purpose. It emphasizes the idea of reaching a spiritual pinnacle, similar to the enlightenment associated with the Crown Chakra.

2. Rest and Reflection

- Crown Chakra: This chakra encourages a state of peace and tranquility, promoting rest and spiritual reflection.

- Day 7 Creation: God resting on the seventh day underscores the importance of taking time to reflect and appreciate creation. This moment of stillness aligns with the tranquility that comes from a balanced Crown Chakra.

3. Divine Connection

- Crown Chakra: The Crown Chakra is the gateway to divine consciousness, allowing us to connect with higher realms and the universe.

- Day 7 Creation: The act of resting signifies a deep connection to the divine, illustrating that completion is not just about physical work but also about spiritual alignment and connection to a higher purpose.

4. Unity and Oneness

- Crown Chakra: This chakra embodies the understanding of unity and the interconnectedness of all beings.

- Day 7 Creation: The completion of creation reflects the idea of oneness with the universe. It encourages us to see ourselves as part of a larger whole, recognizing our interconnectedness with all of creation.

5. Spiritual Awakening

- Crown Chakra: Associated with spiritual awakening, higher consciousness, and awareness beyond the physical realm.

- Day 7 Creation: This day serves as a reminder of the importance of spiritual rest and renewal, allowing for a deeper understanding of our purpose and existence. It invites us to embrace spiritual practices that awaken our consciousness.

The Crown Chakra aligns with Day 7 of Creation through its focus on completion, spiritual fulfillment, and connection to the divine. The act of resting after creation highlights the importance of reflection and the attainment of a higher consciousness. By nurturing our Crown Chakra, we can foster a deeper connection to our spiritual selves and the universe, allowing us to appreciate the beauty and interconnectedness of all life. This alignment emphasizes the value of spiritual growth and the understanding that our existence is part of a greater divine plan.

Day 7 Reincarnation

The seventh day of creation, where God finishes His work and rests, holds deep significance in relation to the process of reincarnation, particularly when viewed through the lens of the birth of a child. Here are several correlations that illustrate this relationship:

1. Completion and Fulfillment: On the seventh day, God completes His creation, signifying a state of fulfillment and harmony. In the context of reincarnation, the birth of a child represents the culmination of a soul's journey through previous lifetimes, bringing with it the wisdom, experiences, and lessons learned. Just as God's work is complete, the child embodies the potential of the soul to manifest its unique purpose in the physical realm.

2. Rest and Reflection: God's rest on the seventh day symbolizes a time for reflection and contemplation. This parallels the birth of a child, which invites families and communities to pause and reflect on the continuity of life and the cycle of existence. The arrival of a new life encourages individuals to consider their own journeys, their spiritual growth, and the legacy they wish to impart to the next generation.

3. Sacredness of Life: The seventh day is sanctified as a holy day, highlighting the importance of rest and spiritual rejuvenation. The birth of a child is similarly a sacred event, marking a new beginning and the potential for spiritual evolution. This connection underscores the idea that every birth is a divine gift and a continuation of the cycle of life, deserving of reverence and celebration.

4. New Beginnings: Just as the seventh day marks the conclusion of creation, it also symbolizes new beginnings. The birth of a child signifies a fresh start, a new chapter in the ongoing narrative of the soul's journey. Each new life offers opportunities for growth, learning, and the exploration of love, compassion, and connection, echoing the notion of a new creation.

5. Interconnectedness: The seventh day emphasizes the interconnectedness of all creation. Similarly, the birth of a child reflects the profound connections among generations, communities, and the universe. Each child brings with it the accumulated experiences of past lives, weaving together the threads of familial and spiritual lineage, fostering a sense of unity and belonging.

6. Restoration and Renewal: God's rest symbolizes a time for restoration and renewal, much like the process of reincarnation. The birth of a child offers the opportunity for families and societies to rejuvenate their values, traditions, and hopes for the future. It serves as a reminder that life is cyclical, with each generation bringing forth the potential for healing and growth.

7. Potential for Growth: The seventh day is a reminder of the divine potential within all of creation. In the same vein, the birth of a child is a celebration of the potential that lies within each new soul. Each child carries the seeds of possibility, ready to explore their purpose, make choices, and contribute to the world, reflecting the ongoing journey of spiritual evolution.

8. Legacy and Continuity: Just as God's creation is an ongoing narrative, so too is the process of reincarnation. The birth of a child symbolizes the continuation of legacy—values, teachings, and experiences passed down through generations. This continuity fosters a sense of responsibility for parents and communities to nurture and guide the child, ensuring that the lessons of the past inform the future.

The seventh day of creation and the birth of a child in the process of reincarnation share profound connections that illuminate the cycles of life, the sacredness of existence, and the potential for spiritual growth. Both signify a state of fulfillment, reflection, and renewal, emphasizing the interconnectedness of all beings and the divine potential within each new life. This day serves as a reminder that every birth is not just an ending but a new beginning in the timeless journey of the soul.

Day 7 Nuanced

Crown Chakra (Sahasrara): A Nuanced Perspective in Relation to Creation and Reincarnation

The Crown Chakra, or Sahasrara, is the seventh energy center in the chakra system, symbolizing our connection to the divine, higher consciousness, and the universal source of all creation. It represents the culmination of spiritual growth, where individual identity merges with the greater whole. In the context of the creation story and the process of reincarnation, the Crown Chakra embodies profound themes of unity, enlightenment, and the return to the source. Here are some nuanced perspectives on this relationship:

1. Unity with the Divine Source

- Connection to God: The creation story begins with God as the singular source of all existence. Similarly, the Crown Chakra represents our spiritual connection to this divine source. In the reincarnation process, realizing this connection can inspire a deeper understanding of our purpose and the lessons we are meant to learn in each lifetime. Just as God created the universe, each soul is a unique expression of that divine essence.

2. Enlightenment and Spiritual Awakening

- Culmination of the Journey: The Crown Chakra is often associated with enlightenment and the realization of one's true nature. In the context of reincarnation, the journey of the soul is one of continual growth and awakening. Each lifetime presents opportunities for learning, and when we reach a higher state of consciousness, we can better understand the purpose behind our experiences. This aligns with the idea of creation as an ongoing process, with every incarnation contributing to our spiritual evolution.

3. Returning to the Source

Cycle of Creation and Rebirth: Just as the creation story narrates the unfolding of the universe, the Crown Chakra embodies the cyclical nature of existence. The process of reincarnation is akin to returning to the divine source, where we ultimately merge back into unity with the cosmos. Understanding this cyclical relationship helps us appreciate the lessons of each life and the importance of spiritual growth as we progress towards our ultimate return to the source.

4. Transcendence of the Ego

- Beyond Individual Identity: The Crown Chakra invites us to transcend the limitations of the ego and recognize our interconnectedness with all beings. In the creation narrative, God creates humanity in His image, suggesting a shared essence. In reincarnation, the ego may be tied to specific identities and life experiences, but the Crown Chakra encourages us to look beyond this individuality to understand the shared spiritual journey we all undertake. This shift in perspective fosters compassion and empathy, allowing us to connect with others on a deeper level.

5. Integration of Experiences

- Synthesizing Lessons Across Lifetimes: The Crown Chakra facilitates the integration of lessons learned throughout various incarnations. Much like the creation story's unfolding narrative, our soul's journey involves gathering insights and wisdom from each lifetime. By connecting to the Crown Chakra, we can better understand how past experiences shape our current life, allowing for deeper healing and growth.

6. Divine Guidance and Intuition

- Receiving Spiritual Wisdom: The Crown Chakra serves as a conduit for divine guidance and intuition. In the context of the creation story, the voice of God provides direction and purpose. Similarly, by nurturing our Crown Chakra, we open ourselves to receiving insights and guidance from higher realms. This connection is crucial during the reincarnation process, as it helps us align with our soul's mission and navigate the complexities of life with greater clarity.

7. Collective Consciousness

- Awareness of the Whole: The Crown Chakra symbolizes our connection to the collective consciousness of humanity. This aligns with the idea that every creation contributes to the whole. In reincarnation, understanding our place within this collective can enhance our sense of belonging and purpose. By recognizing that we are part of something greater, we can cultivate a sense of responsibility towards others and the world around us.

8. Celebration of Life's Journey

- Embracing the Infinite Cycle: The Crown Chakra encourages us to celebrate the beauty of life's journey and the cycles of creation and rebirth. Each incarnation is an opportunity to explore, learn, and grow. By embracing this perspective, we can approach our experiences with gratitude and openness, recognizing that every moment is a gift that contributes to our spiritual evolution.

The Crown Chakra serves as a profound bridge between the creation story and the reincarnational journey, illuminating our connection to the divine, the importance of spiritual awakening, and the cyclical nature of existence. By nurturing this energy center, we can deepen our understanding of our place in the universe and the interconnectedness of all beings. The Crown Chakra invites us to transcend individual limitations, integrate our experiences, and celebrate the infinite journey of the soul. Through this lens, we come to appreciate the divine purpose behind creation and reincarnation, ultimately guiding us toward greater unity, enlightenment, and fulfillment.

Epilogue

As we close the pages of this exploration, we find ourselves standing at the intersection of creation, reincarnation, and the intricate dance of our chakras. The journey through these profound themes has illuminated not just the ancient narratives that shape our understanding of existence, but also the deeply personal experiences that define our spiritual evolution.

In the act of creation, we have seen the unfolding of a universe that mirrors our own inner landscapes. Each day of creation, each step in the cycle of life, resonates with the stages of our personal growth and transformation. Just as the world was meticulously formed, so too are our souls crafted through a tapestry of experiences, emotions, and lessons learned across lifetimes.

The concept of reincarnation invites us to embrace the idea that life is not a linear journey but a cyclical one. Each life we live offers us a chance to evolve, to learn, and to become more aligned with our true selves. This perspective reshapes how we view challenges and setbacks, transforming them into opportunities for growth. We are reminded that every moment, every decision, and every interaction contributes to the ongoing story of our spirit.

Equally, the exploration of the chakras provides us with a powerful framework for understanding our emotional, mental, and spiritual well-being. Each energy center, from the grounding essence of the root chakra to the expansive wisdom of the crown, serves as a portal to deeper self-awareness and connection to the universe. As we navigate our lives, we can utilize this knowledge to cultivate balance, harmony, and clarity, allowing our true essence to shine forth.

As you step away from this book, I encourage you to carry these insights into your daily life. Reflect on how the narratives of creation and reincarnation manifest in your own experiences. Consider the ways in which your chakras influence your emotional states, relationships, and personal growth. Allow this understanding to guide you in nurturing your spirit, fostering resilience, and seeking out the beauty in the cycles of life.

In a world that often feels chaotic and overwhelming, remember that you are part of a grand story—one that is continually unfolding. Embrace your role as a creator of your reality, and trust in the journey of your soul. Each breath, each moment, is a gift, a chance to create, to learn, and to connect.

Thank you for joining me on this enlightening journey. May you walk forward with courage and curiosity, ever open to the wonders of creation and the infinite possibilities that lie within you. Your story is a vital part of the collective narrative, and it is one that deserves to be lived fully and authentically.

With love and light,

Alex

About Alex Telman

Alex Telman is a renowned Spiritual Healer based in Brisbane, Australia. He is celebrated for his profound influence on the mind and spirit, he was a pioneering leader in the self-help movement of the 1980s. Alex has dedicated over 45 years to empowering individuals to transform their lives through healing and inspiration.

From an early age, Alex's fascination with the Spirit guided him toward a path of deep insight, where he skillfully blends traditional spiritual practices with contemporary therapeutic techniques. His impressive academic credentials include degrees in Law, Arts, Hypnotherapy, and Education, providing him with a comprehensive understanding of psychic phenomena and the spiritual dimensions of everyday life. His diverse clientele ranges from natural health practitioners and spiritual healers to celebrities and business leaders, all seeking his unique wisdom and guidance.

Beyond his healing practice, Alex is a prolific poet whose works encompass sonnets, sestinas, and modern poetic forms. His poetry captures the essence of life in both urban and rural settings, delving into the psychological and philosophical depths of the human experience. Recognized for their profound insight, his poems weave realism with emotional richness, offering readers a deeper understanding of life's complexities.

As an esteemed author and dynamic public speaker, Alex masterfully combines his expertise in the fields of spiritual healing, transformative psychology and poetry, to inspire others toward greater clarity and self-awareness. His commitment to community engagement fosters personal and collective transformation, ensuring that each client receives the care and attention they deserve. Alex Telman's journey is a testament to the transformative power of healing and self-expression, illuminating pathways to richer, more meaningful lives.

In Brisbane's heart, where city lights embrace,
A spirit thrives where timeless truths entwine—
Alex Telman, whose quest for light and grace
Unites the ancient wisdom with the modern line.
Since youth, the Spirit's call was pure and bright,
A journey through the mists of deepened lore;
In realms of arcane art and healing's light,
He navigates where hidden truths implore.
His sonnets chart the human heart's vast sweep,
Where light and dark in delicate balance play—
Each line a beacon in the night's deep sleep,
Unveiling depths where inner truths hold sway.
A healer's gift, a poet's rare finesse,
In Alex's work, both mind and soul find rest.

Front Cover: William Blake – God Creating the Universe

What resonated with me about this painting is its portrayal of Creation as a thoughtful and intricate endeavor—one that, paradoxically for the Divine Creator, involves the use of a scientific instrument.

It told me that there was more to this story than meets the eye and here was an inquiry I should follow. I have.

In the realm of Western culture, particularly in art, literature, and critical thought, to me William Blake stands as a monumental figure. I hope you enjoy his work.

- *Alex*

Don't miss out!

Visit the website below and you can sign up to receive emails whenever Alex Telman publishes a new book. There's no charge and no obligation.

https://books2read.com/r/B-A-YBSCC-ADGCF

BOOKS 2 READ

Connecting independent readers to independent writers.

Did you love *The Truth Behind the Creation Story*? Then you should read *Legends and Lessons*[1] by Alex Telman!

[2]

Unlock the Mysteries of Myth and Legend: An Epic Journey Through Time.

Dive into the enchanting world of myths and legends with this compelling collection, "Legends and Lessons: 36 Myths Unveiled". This book invites you to explore profound truths through beautifully crafted poetry.

Each myth—transformed into original poems—paints vivid imagery and breathes life into timeless stories that have shaped cultures for centuries. From the fiery defiance of Prometheus to the tragic love of Orpheus and Eurydice, every poem serves as a gateway to explore the depths of human experience, revealing the wisdom embedded within our shared narratives.

But this book offers more than just poetry; each story is paired with insightful explanations of the life lessons that resonate through the ages. Discover the consequences of hubris in the tale of Icarus, or the enduring power of love

---

1. https://books2read.com/u/4X5yAv
2. https://books2read.com/u/4X5yAv

and sacrifice in the saga of Isis and Osiris. Each legend acts as a mirror, reflecting our struggles, aspirations, and the complexities of life itself.

Imagine immersing yourself in the tales of Hercules as he conquers his labors, or journeying alongside Jason and the Argonauts on their quest for the Golden Fleece. Experience the struggle against fate in the haunting story of Sisyphus, and embrace the renewal symbolized by the Phoenix. Each narrative is an exploration of humanity—its triumphs and failures, its dreams and despairs.

"Legends and Lessons" is perfect for readers of all ages—students, educators, and anyone who seeks inspiration and connection through the art of storytelling. It ignites the imagination and encourages reflection, making it an ideal companion for book clubs, classrooms, or personal libraries.

Join me on this poetic odyssey, where the ancient echoes of our past meet the modern heart. Whether you are a lifelong lover of myths or just beginning your journey, this collection promises to captivate your mind and spirit.

Don't miss your chance to own a piece of literary art that celebrates the eternal dance between humanity and its legends. "Legends and Lessons: 36 Myths Unveiled" is more than a book; it's a journey through time, a celebration of culture, and a guide to the lessons that shape our lives.

Order your copy today and let the wisdom of the ancients inspire you!

Read more at www.AlexTelman.com.

www.ingramcontent.com/pod-product-compliance
Lightning Source LLC
LaVergne TN
LVHW010457160826
845677LV00012B/2518

* 9 7 9 8 2 2 7 3 2 7 4 2 0 *